"Dr. Matt's book is not some textbook description... It is a celebration of doing, acting, living. Dominating!... If you put in the time and effort and conquer this very common fear, then you'll realize that perhaps other seemingly unattainable things – really aren't... He didn't present an unrealistic picture... that every single presentation will end with a standing ovation. He focused on what you can control – your preparation, dedication and attitude. And your outfit."
– **K. Berrada**

"I received my copy of the book on Tuesday, and by Wednesday I was done. It was one of the smoothest, easiest books I have had the pleasure of reading. The stretch exercises he assigns are just enough to make you feel guilty if you don't do them. I have my first scheduled for next week because he says (paraphrasing here) if you wait until you're ready... you'll never do anything." – **Tina Muegge**

"This actually may BE the best public speaking book! This book is extremely well written, clear, and concise, while still giving enough detail and wisdom to prepare you for your next public speaking role – whether it's just giving a motivational talk to your tee-ball team, or delivering a large-scale presentation to heads of state!"
– **E. Gonzalez**

The *Best* Public Speaking Book

2nd Edition

by Matt Deaton, Ph.D.

Audiobook ISBN 978-1-951677-12-1

e-Book ISBN 978-1-951677-02-2

Hardcover ISBN 978-1-951677-01-5

Paperback ISBN 978-1-951677-00-8

Published by Notaed Press

Cover design by Paula Ambrosio of paulambrosio.com

Copyediting of original edition
by Hayley Shepherd of Miss Pelt's Literacy Services

General editorial consultation on original edition
by Roberta Israeloff and Melody Gonzalez

Interior design of original edition
By John Richard Stephens

Proofing of second edition
by Barbara Carringer

NOTAEDPRESS

For the ambitious rookie.

You got this.

CONTENTS

Chapter One: Swimmers Must Swim – 1

Part I: The Three Commandments of Public Speaking – 15

Chapter Two: Commandments Preview – 17

Chapter Three: Commandment I: Know Thy Material – 23

Chapter Four: Commandment II: Be Thyself – 55

Chapter Five: Commandment III: Practice – 65

Part II: Developing Stage Presence – 75

Chapter Six: Conquering Nervousness – 77

Chapter Seven: Involving Your Audience – 105

Chapter Eight: Handling a Tough Crowd – 115

Part III: Mastering The Mechanics – 127

Chapter Nine: Physical Delivery – 129

Chapter Ten: Oral Delivery – 141

Chapter Eleven: If You Must Use a Script... – 153

Chapter Twelve: Using Technology – 159

Part IV: Always Improving – 175

Chapter Thirteen: Less Reading, More Speaking – 177

Chapter Fourteen: The Commitment to Get Better – 195

Chapter Fifteen: Mindset Revisited – 203

Chapter Sixteen: Paid to Speak? – 215

Chapter Seventeen: Tell Them What You've Told Them – 227

More Books by Matt Deaton – 238

Chapter One

SWIMMERS MUST SWIM

You can read the best swimming books, memorize the strokes, and even air-swim on land. But until you get in the water, you'll never experience the joy of swimming, nor the satisfaction of knowing how.

The same is true for speaking. You can read the best speaking books, memorize the delivery techniques, and even rehearse in private. But until you get on that stage, you'll never experience the joy of public speaking, nor the satisfaction of knowing how.

This is why we need you in front of an audience—any audience—as soon and as often as possible. Speaking on small, informal topics for small, informal audiences (in the shallow end, with arm floaties) is fine at first. But know that the goal isn't to simply learn about public speaking, but to do it, and do it well.

If you've been tiptoeing around the diving board, procrasti-studying rather than taking the plunge, fair warning that your stage-dodging days are numbered. However, know that by the time we get to the stretch assignments in chapter thirteen, you'll be armed with everything you need to succeed (mentally, technically, physically) and more.

Now take a deep breath (in through the nose, out through the mouth), and relax. Public speaking isn't as hard as we've been led to believe. You got this.

SPEAKING = IDEA TRANSFER

Once upon a time, I overcomplicated public speaking. Big time. Seeing smooth talkers on TV and online (especially those TED Talkers), the gap between where I was and where I apparently needed to be seemed too big. No way I could match their eloquence. How'd they even remember all that material?

But if had I known how many doors would open once I could present any idea to any crowd, anywhere, anytime (with a little prep time, anyway), I wouldn't have waited so long to discover the basic truth that public speaking is communication.

Whether it's Linus sharing the true meaning of Christmas, General Patton rallying his troops, or Robin Williams challenging English students to seize the day, speakers have ideas in their heads that they'd like to transfer into the heads of their audience members. Accomplish that basic goal of idea transfer and you're a public speaking success. Ta-da!

Public speaking is a *special kind* of communication, with special conventions, expectations, challenges and opportunities. And there's definitely a craft and art to be mastered. But don't let anyone—including me—make it any more complicated than it is. Public speaking is communication—that's it.

TELL THEM WHAT YOU'RE ABOUT TO TELL THEM

There are three ironclad rules that presenters break at their own risk. Embrace them, and you can look and feel like a rock star on stage. Ignore them, you can still look and feel like a rock star—just a washed-up, out-of-shape rock star struggling through a hangover.

These Three Commandments of Public Speaking: Know Thy Material, Be Thyself, and Practice, are the focus of Part I, with a chapter devoted to each. They're commandments for a reason, so pay attention.

If you're like I used to be, even reading about public speaking makes you antsy. That's why we'll begin Part II:

Developing Stage Presence by slaying the stage fright dragon. Truly knowing your material, being yourself and practicing will eliminate 70-80% of public speaking nervousness. (Yes, really.) But to take care of the rest we'll add stage-empowering techniques on mindset, posture, and wardrobe, as well as a visualization exercise from hypnotist Paul McKenna.

We'll also practice the Urban Honey Badger, a self-defense drill that will boost your assertiveness both on stage and off. (That's an urban honey badger on the cover—ain't he cute?) General timidity is often a root cause of speaking anxiety, so while repelling imaginary bad guys (and mauling their faces when forced) is an unorthodox way to build stage presence, it works. The goal isn't to simply *survive* on stage, but to replace stage fright with stage dominance—to go from feeling like prey, to feeling like a predator, or at least a self-assured bipedal omnivore.

In chapters seven and eight we'll cover how to handle tough crowds, be they withdrawn or aggressive, as well as how to engage and keep your audience involved. We'll discuss how to brush off frowny faces, how to prevent the mood from going sour, and even how to shut down hecklers (spoiler: pepper spray). Hecklers are rare, but it's good to have a plan should one pop up (hint: buy pepper spray).

In Part III: *Mastering the Mechanics* we'll cover the technical aspects of physical and oral delivery—how to tailor your silent message to win your audience's respect and make you feel good (though not as good as pepper spraying a heckler), how to project your voice and stop mumbling ("Rubber baby buggy bumpers..."), as well as when and when *not* to use a lectern.

We'll also discuss how to use a script on the rare occasion that doing so is appropriate (spoiler: scripts are the devil), and how to incorporate technology—how to use PowerPoint as an illustrative aid rather than a mind-numbing crutch, how to get comfortable with a microphone, and even how to present remotely via speakerphone or Zoom (tip: assume remote audience members are scrolling through Facebook... on the potty).

We'll begin part IV: *Always Improving* with chapter thirteen, "Less Reading, More Speaking." There you'll deliver a series of confidence-building presentations that include a "checkout speech" (literally practicing a mini-talk on an unwitting cashier), a library volunteer assignment, and possibly even open mic night at the local comedy club. You'll even get a chance to make a YouTube vid and share it with me for a little feedback.

These assignments may sound scary now. But you'll be prepared by the time we get there, and in chapter fourteen we'll cover how to grow from every talk you give—no opportunity to improve overlooked. (I once tried to tell jokes at an art studio variety show, and bombed badly. Turned out to be one of the most instructive presentations of my life.)

Then we'll re-focus on mindset, you'll learn how to overcome the evil of perfectionism, how to rid yourself of subconscious sabotage, and how to view small struggles as invaluable chances to get better. Notice the pattern: study, speak, improve, repeat.

In addition to the Three Commandments section, the YouTuber assignment, the "handling tough crowds" chapter and other scattered improvements, new in this 2nd edition is a chapter on the speaking business, chapter sixteen, "Paid to Speak?" There you'll learn the basics of becoming a semi-pro (getting paid to do something once terrifying is super cool), enriched by the advice of Alan Weiss, Brian Tracy, Fredrik Haren and Patrick Schwerdtfeger, professionals who know a thing or two about the biz. Depending on your experience, this may sound crazy. But I felt the same way, so don't rule it out.

Last, we'll recap all you've learned, glean some parting wisdom from a gum-chewing sports legend and a rough-riding president, and recommit to speaking rather than simply reading about speaking. Each step of the way, remember the not-so-secret secret that just as swimmers must swim, speakers must speak. Start getting used to the idea that you're already a confident, competent speaker, envision your ideal speaking self kicking butt on stage, and get ready to make that vision a reality.

A REPEATABLE PATH

Just as your audiences should be the heroes of your talks, you're the hero of this book. But so you're reassured I know what I'm talking about, here's my journey in a nutshell.

Public speaking didn't come naturally. I wasn't captain of my high school's debate team (not that my small-town school had a debate team), I didn't take my first public speaking class until my mid-twenties, and my mom is still amazed to see her once shy son speaking to hundreds with poise and skill. Pausing a comedy show to hand-deliver her a rose during a Mother's Day performance was especially fun—a memory we wouldn't share if I had continued to run from my potential.

It took me a while to warm to the idea. But once I realized how public speaking was an essential success skill, fear gave way to ambition. Today my stage successes include:

- Speaking from a spot where a US president had recently spoken (the only time I've gotten dry mouth on stage—politics aside, following Obama, even if it was weeks later, caused my belly butterflies to multiply, crawl up my throat and drink my saliva)

- Being entrusted to inspire 300 or so K-12 teachers at the beginning of the 2015 and 2017 schoolyears (after being a bit of a juvenile delinquent, this was a special honor—put *that* in my permanent record)
- Speaking at a conference near Times Square (in a fancy ballroom with crystal chandeliers—reminded me of the Ghostbusters scene where they trap Slimer)
- Hosting my high school class's first reunion (if you've attended yours, you know why this is impressive)
- Delivering custom public speaking workshops for hospital staff, traveling inspections teams, office workers, Toastmasters, colleagues, debate teams and students from junior high through college
- Opening ethics bowls at American University in DC and the University of Tennessee, and touting the discourse-elevating benefits of ethics bowls at conferences from California to Ohio
- Leading live webinars for national and even global audiences (fielding questions from attendees in India, Europe, and places I couldn't find on a map while presenting online for the Project Management Institute was especially cool)
- Leading a Zoom-based training for students in China, and opening another for students in Australia (the Chinese students spoke English, but many with

Australian accents, which was an odd dialect layering for sure)

- Eulogizing a high school friends funeral (Jerome, may you rest in peace), and an uncle's "celebration of life" (followed by a square dance—John wouldn't have had it any other way)

- Emceeing a mentor's retirement party (happy retirement, Glenn!)

- Keynoting an achievement banquet for my county's top high school graduates (researching, I learned that one of our alumni is engineering self-driving cars in England—way to make us proud, Joe Gettinger!)

- Posting dozens of mini-talks on philosophy and ethics at YouTube.com/MattDeatonPhD (Marxism vs. Libertarianism, abortion ethics in the coming age of artificial wombs, whether we should fear or celebrate Super Artificial Intelligence—the usual stuff)

- Presenting on firearms policy, medical ethics, political theory and more at philosophy conferences from St. Louis to St. Augustine

- Keynoting a half dozen or so Veterans Day programs (tip: if you're invited to do one, interview local vets and re-tell their favorite service stories—crowds love local vet service stories)

- Hosting a comedy club during grad school (the host kicks off, closes, and keeps the show moving, and in my case introduces the traveling headliners like a UFC announcer, as in: "Ladies and gentlemen, join me in giving a warm Side Splitters welcome to *Re*-noooooooooo *Colh*er!")

I'm also a student of the craft, and love to read (and apply the better advice of) public speaking authors. Carmine Gallo's *Talk Like TED* is a bestseller for a reason, and highly recommended. The same for Brian Tracy's *Speak to Win*, Scott Berkun's *Confessions of a Public Speaker*, and Patrick Schwerdtfeger's *Keynote Mastery*. Some of their tips are included here (with credit, of course).

In addition to extracurricular keynote speaking, I also lead monthly conference calls, seasonal webinars, and ad hoc online meetings. Some events are constrained ("Cover this specific material, in this specific way, in this specific time"). Some are flexible ("We know you'll do a great job—talk about whatever you like for as long as you want!"). Most are somewhere in between.

My point is that I don't simply write about public speaking. I don't simply coach it. I actively study and do it, with a resume that grows increasingly cooler. Last January I was invited to build a motivational speech around my new book, *Year of the Fighter* (about the time I decided to competitively box and kickbox for my midlife crisis—ouch) for my chamber of commerce's annual member appreciation breakfast. Then an attendee hired me to kickoff a summer work program at a nearby college. A few months later the chamber invited me back to speak at their business appreciation luncheon (repeat customers are a good sign). As of this writing, next Wednesday I'm hosting a speaking workshop for a Toastmasters club (more on Toastmasters in chapter seventeen).

However, I'm not a speaking superstar. *Yet.* In addition to writing, I teach philosophy online (the reason for the YouTube channel), and hold down a day job as a management analyst (the reason for the recurring online/phone meetings). Rather than a jet-setting global keynoting pro *(yet!),* I'm a work in progress. But to go from zero to the list you just read? If I can do it, you can do it. And maybe the fact that I'm still on my way up will make my perspective more relatable, my advice more useful, and my coaching more valuable.

The Target Audience

So if you're here to turn your million-dollar speaking career into a *two*-million-dollar speaking career, awesome. But if you simply want to present your class project without hyperventilating, or deliver the Thanksgiving blessing without choking on your own spit, or brief your boss's boss without peeing your pants, even better. I'm sure pros could learn a thing or two. But this book is for the determined rookie—for people like I used to be—ambitious, but largely clueless, and (if we're honest) a little scared.

Maybe like me, the better you get, the more speaking you'll want to do, especially once your bodily functions are under control. Captivating a live audience—inspiring, enlightening and entertaining to the tune of laughter, smiles and applause—can be addictive.

But regardless of how far you take this, thank you for trusting me to share the joy of public speaking with you. When the once scary becomes fun, that's a nice feeling. And the thought of helping people like you make that transition makes coaching via the written (and spoken) word especially satisfying.

THE TIME IS NOW

People who wait for the perfect moment to get in shape, propose marriage or start their dream business wait until they're dead. Conditions will never be perfect. Whatever the goal, this year is better than next year. Today is better than tomorrow. Now is better than after lunch.

If you wait until you feel completely prepared to give your first (or next) presentation, that moment will never come.

Successful people act *before* they feel fully prepared. This is you, especially when it comes to launching and advancing your speaking journey.

Know that it's going to be worth the effort. Part of the pleasure of realizing your ideal public speaking self comes from the universal recognition that it ain't easy. Everyone knows it's tough (at first). Everyone knows it's scary (at first). So most go to their grave with the regret of never having given it a fair try.

As a result, those of us with the courage to get up there and the determination to get better (the only two traits aspiring speakers need) gain instant respect, with cooler doors opening every time we do it.

So kudos for having the guts. And as your personal style and speaking path begin to reveal themselves, remember not to let anyone (including me) overcomplicate this stuff.

Public speaking is communication. That's it. It's a special kind of communication with special conventions, expectations and opportunities. But still, nothing more than idea transfer. It's going to take stage time to uncover and polish your authentic stage self. But no worries at all. *You got this.*

Key Takeaways

➲ Just as swimmers must swim, **speakers must speak**

➲ Public speaking is **communication**—simple idea transfer

➲ Improving as a speaker takes the **courage** to get up there and the **commitment** to get better—you have both

➲ Successful people act **before** they're fully ready—so let's go!

Part I

The Three
Commandments of
Public Speaking

Chapter Two

COMMANDMENTS
PREVIEW

Follow the Three Commandments of Public Speaking and you can look and feel like Elvis in his prime—mastery, grace, stage dominance. Break them, and you'll look and feel like Fat Elvis after a greasy meal.

Unless Fat Elvis was awesome after a greasy meal... Anyway, you get the idea. Here come the Commandments. Follow them or Elvis's ghost will drip grease on you.

COMMANDMENT I: KNOW THY MATERIAL

If a drill instructor handed you an M-16 rifle and demanded you deliver a presentation on how to clean it five minutes from now, unless you're an ex-Marine or a gun nut, it wouldn't be pretty. You'd feel bewildered, and if you actually tried, would probably spend more time apologizing than teaching.

Now imagine being given three months to prepare, a spare rifle to take home, and access to the best M-16 cleaning how-to materials. Assuming you could overcome any initial firearms ickiness, you could research and practice proper cleaning techniques, reflect on the best way to convey them, and develop a nice interactive talk.

Your opening skit would get your audience in the rifle-cleaning mood (perhaps a story involving zombies and an inopportune misfire), your contrast of the M-16 with the more simply designed AK-47 would confirm your authority (M-16s are more accurate, but AK-47s more reliable—you recommend a well-oiled U.S. model when trying to prevent becoming the undead's lunch), and your recap would leave your audience sure they could maintain their own machine gun, should the zombie apocalypse befall us.

By the time the presentation arrived, there would be no question in your mind, nor in the minds of your audience members, that you'd done your homework. You'd be clear, thorough, organized and interactive. You'd feel good beforehand, great during, and proud afterwards. You'd discover firsthand how delivering a talk you've mastered isn't stressful, but fun. Especially when zombies and ammunition are involved.

We'll cover how to clarify and organize your material next chapter. But for now, commit to always *knowing* what you're talking about. That alone will eliminate a great deal of nervousness, and make you a far more effective communicator.

And if you're not a topic expert when you receive a speaking assignment, no worries. You'll become an expert (relative to your audience, anyway) during prep.

COMMANDMENT II: BE THYSELF

Imagine a time you pretended to be someone you're not. You wanted to impress an employer, an in-law, Officer Tackleberry at a traffic stop, and put on a mask you thought would appear more knowledgeable, proper, law-abiding.

Do you remember feeling ashamed, skittish, and resentful? Those are the predictable side effects of fakery. And they're the exact opposite of the sincere, connected dynamic we want with our audiences.

People can sense when you're not being yourself, which will cost you credibility, as well as respect. (Officer Tackleberry shows no mercy regardless, so fake away with him.) That's why a big part of realizing your potential as a speaker involves uncovering and polishing your authentic stage self.

Figuring out what that looks and feels like will take stage time. And it's likely to evolve. But to the extent we can mold your unique speaking style into something you're proud of, something that's unmistakably *you*, you'll feel better on stage, your audience will be more likely to like and listen to you, and you'll be that much more effective.

We'll focus on this in chapter four. For now, simply commit to being *you* on stage.

COMMANDMENT III: PRACTICE

When audience members offer praise after one of my talks, they're always surprised when I tell them I rehearsed at least a dozen times before going live. *Of course* I presented to stuffed animals in my living room so I could practice eye contact (unicorn eyes are solid black and creepy, but they're still eyes). *Of course* I experimented with ten different intros before deciding which was best. *Of course* I came on site, connected my laptop to the projector and ran through the whole thing the day before to ensure my technology wouldn't catch fire, envisioning an appreciative audience smiling back (with brown, blue, green, non-creepy eyes). That's what professionals who care do.

Pretending that I winged it might be more impressive. But it would dismiss the hard work that happens before every quality talk I give.

Talks that are less important don't warrant as much prep. But to the extent you've rehearsed, and to the extent that you've rehearsed as you intend to perform (standing if you'll be standing, using a mic if you'll be using a mic, walking around if you'll be walking around, clicking through your slides if you'll be using slides), you'll feel and actually *be* better.

Rehearsal is when it all comes together, the edge that distinguishes serious speakers (who get invited back) from bunglers (who don't). When you tweak your talk each time through—making it a little clearer, with transitions that are a little smoother, with examples that are a little more potent, with exercises that are a little more engaging, in a way that feels a little more authentic—that's when presentations (and speakers) go from good to great.

We'll unpack Commandment Three in chapter five. But we begin with coming to know your material through careful study and message development. What follows, just like everything, is customizable. You be the judge of what's most useful for your purposes. Except for the Three Commandments, which Elvis's ghost demands you follow.

Key Takeaways

➲ Know Thy Material (you're an **expert** and **teacher**—prepare accordingly)

➲ Be Thyself (embrace your authentic, polished *stage* self, which **will reveal itself** with experience and **evolve** over time)

➲ Practice (as you intend to **deliver**)

Chapter Three

COMMANDMENT I: KNOW THY MATERIAL

Whether you're talking about widget fasteners, batting averages or Book X of Plato's *Republic*, whether you're delivering a speech to an auditorium, a boardroom or a Cub Scout pack, knowing what you're talking about is *the* key to effective public speaking. When you know what you're talking about, everything—and I mean *everything*—improves. When you don't know what you're talking about, everything—and I mean *everything*—gets worse.

As a professor, when I've taken the time to study, organize, and internalize my lesson plan, I've been able to illustrate points with impromptu examples, diagram interconnected concepts on the board, and answer tough questions with ease. (Well, they're philosophical questions, so maybe not with ease, but with more ease than had I shown up unprepared.) However, on the rare occasion that I've tried to lecture without adequate prep, even when I *thought* I understood the material, I've struggled to articulate my points, stumbled through crude explanations, and worried the whole time a student would ask a question I couldn't answer. Not fun.

That's why knowing your material not only impacts the content of your presentation, but the quality of your delivery. On the days I knew my stuff, and *knew* I knew my stuff, the confidence that followed felt great. But on days I didn't know my stuff, and *knew* I didn't know my stuff, the anxiety that followed made me feel terrible. Feeling crummy inside ruined my delivery, as well as my students' experience. One third of the class would look confused, one third would look frustrated, and the other third would look out the window.

Studying, organizing and streamlining your material takes time. But the key that distinguishes great presenters from OK presenters is intelligent message development. You can be confident, well-spoken, and look fabulous. But if your message is confusing and your core ideas buried under distracting fluff, your audience won't learn much, even if they're superficially impressed. "She sure was a smooth talker. What was she was talking about, again?"

The good news is that you can develop a clear and memorable presentation, and come to thoroughly *know* your material, via seven easy steps:[1]

1. Clarify your goals and sketch an outline

2. Embrace your role as expert and teacher

3. Consider your audience

4. Download and unpack your core message

5. Logically arrange your ideas

6. Backfill with analogies, examples & stories

7. Revise using Zinsser's Four Principles

1 CLARIFY YOUR GOALS & SKETCH AN OUTLINE

Once you've committed to give a talk, ask yourself: What's the purpose? What do I want my audience to understand, accept, remember or do? What are my draft key points, what visual aids might I use, how can I actively involve the audience?

Speaking coach and achievement guru Brian Tracy calls this initial brainstorming phase the "Down Dump." Imagine

---

[1] *Seven* steps?! I know, that's about four too many. But give it a shot, and if you start getting bogged down, skip ahead to the last three, then review the Key Takeaways at the end. However, this is the longest, most technical chapter in the book, so if you can tough this one out, smooth sailing awaits.

what would need to happen for your talk to go perfectly, then capture everything that comes to mind. Messy is fine. Disorganized is fine. Just capture. Once it's out, *then* switch into organization mode.

Tracy suggests drawing five circles on a sheet of paper and bucketing your ideas based where they best fit—opening, close, or under key points A, B or C. Rather than circles, I'll often use PowerPoint. I'll title slides and type in placeholder details to revise later, such as "insert map of ethics bowl expansion here" or "F-22 Raptor combat takeoff clip here."

I've also organized talks using tiered lists. For example, if I were planning a pre-game speech for my old tee ball team, I'd first type out our goals for the season:

- ➲ Have fun
- ➲ Make friends
- ➲ Build confidence
- ➲ Learn tee ball basics

Then I'd think about what I could say and do during the ninety seconds between warming up and taking the field that would help bring those goals about:

- ➲ Have fun: Lead team cheer (Go, Panthers!)
- ➲ Make friends: Exchange high fives
- ➲ Build confidence: Compliment each player on one area of improvement
- ➲ Learn tee ball basics: Reinforce a tip from practice

For the final draft we can remove the background goals, and no outline is complete without a proper ordering. The team cheer comes at the very end, and we should exchange high fives before the individual encouragement and the tip from practice. Plus, a little more detail would be nice, so I should add a few sub-bullets. How about:

I. Exchange high fives

II. Compliment each player on one area of improvement:
    A. Andrew's patience
    B. Lexi's swing
    C. Miles's defense
    D. Amelia's speed
    E. Justin's throwing
    F. Malia's focus

III. Reinforce a tip from practice:
    A. Do not hit me with the bat

IV. Lead team cheer (Go, Panthers!)

We'll talk more about ordering and fleshing out your ideas in a moment. The point here is to clarify your goals and sketch an outline consistent with them as soon as possible. As Stephen Covey puts it, when we "begin with the end in mind" we have a much better chance of arriving somewhere we want, and a much better time getting there.

2 EMBRACE YOUR ROLE AS EXPERT & TEACHER

It doesn't matter if I'm discussing *The Giving Tree* with third graders, teaching awareness and avoidance to self-defense students, or briefing executives on business ethics—presentations go better when I think of myself as an expert and teacher.

Adopting the expert mindset sets the expectation that by the time you present you'll know what you're talking about. And thinking of yourself as a teacher—whether you'll be presenting in an official classroom setting or not—reinforces the fact that it's on you to get those ideas into the heads of your audience members. The result is that you'll show up much better prepared, much more comfortable than you'd otherwise be, and your audience will learn much more than they otherwise would.

Note the importance of being both expert *and* teacher. We've all known experts who were poor teachers, and charismatic, passionate teachers who didn't know their stuff. Our aim is to embody the best of both—to have something to convey, as well as the ability to convey it.

If you happen to be presenting on a topic you know little about, the beauty of public speaking is that studying it and organizing your ideas will make you a quasi-expert in the process. The adage, "If you want to master a subject, teach it" is true.

Since you're now cool with being a teacher, here's a secret: You can teach almost anyone almost anything by following three simple steps: relate, unpack, and reinforce. Whatever your topic, connect it to something your audience already understands, explain how the two are similar, and clarify the nuances.

When my oldest son was three, he asked me to teach him about hockey. So I related it to a game he already understood and enjoyed—soccer. "Hockey, Son, is soccer with sticks... on ice." The soccer connection enabled him to envision goals on either end of an icy playing area, through which players would attempt to knock... *something* with sticks.

I explained that that something was a "puck"—a smooth rock shaped like a big Oreo cookie—and that the players wore special shoes similar to his roller skates, except with metal blades on the bottom instead of wheels. In just a few seconds he knew a whole lot about hockey due to connections to things he already understood: soccer, cookies, and roller skates.

Similarly, at the beginning of this book I helped you appreciate the importance of stage time for new speakers by relating it to the importance of pool time for new swimmers. You can teach almost anyone almost anything this same way— by relating new knowledge to existing knowledge.

However, people learn differently. Some learn best by hearing, some by seeing, others by focusing on the big picture, and others by examining the smaller parts. Education experts call these the verbal, visual, global and analytic learning styles.

As a professor, I've sometimes been asked by the university to give my students a survey at the beginning of a new semester to assess their learning styles. These are more for my students' benefit than mine, for I always have some who are dominant verbal (learn best via the spoken word), some who are dominant visual (need images), some who are dominant global (prefer big-picture explanations), and some who are dominant analytic (crave the finer details). Since I'm responsible for teaching everyone—not simply those who prefer the most common learning style—it's best to engage every style every class.

Having to cover all four styles might sound a little intimidating. But most of us do it automatically. Just imagine any coach giving any halftime locker room speech. What do you see? Is he explaining his strategy for the second half with his gravelly voice (verbal)? Or is he drawing X's and O's on a dusty chalkboard (visual)? Is he talking about high-level strategy (global)? Or is he also giving guidance to specific players (analytic)? Chances are good that he's engaging all four learning styles without even trying. Chances are good that you will, too.

You won't always have a chalkboard at your disposal. But you will always have your voice, and you can use it to paint images in the minds of your visual learners (like I just painted that locker room scene for you).

So accept and remember that as a public speaker you're an expert and a teacher. Study your subject, be able to relate it to something your audience already understands, and keep those learning styles in mind. But don't sweat them too much. You're likely to address all four without even trying.

3 CONSIDER YOUR AUDIENCE

People are people. So long as you clearly communicate a logically arranged message with good examples that connect new ideas to ideas they already understand, any human should be able to follow. However, the exact language you use, how deeply you delve into your subject, your areas of emphasis and your examples do need customization.

Say you're giving a thirty-minute presentation on rocket boosters. If you'll be speaking to kindergarteners, you might begin with a group countdown to get their attention: "Three, two, one, BLAST OFF!" then pass around a model rocket for the kids to examine (and inevitably break). You could explain that "The body of a rocket is a cylinder, like Oscar from Sesame Street's unfortunate trash can house." And given their short attention spans, you might present for five minutes and spend the other twenty-five helping them build cardboard models of their own (which you could then accidentally break).

If your audience is chemical engineering graduate students, your explanations can be more abstract and complex, and your learning goals more ambitious. Feel free to cite fancy equations (engineering students love fancy equations). And if your audience is somewhere in-between—perhaps bright laypeople like us—just consider what you can expect them to know and adjust.

It's also smart to consider what your audience desires to get out of your talk. For example, if I were a baseball team manager given thirty minutes to brief the owner on equipment needs, I wouldn't bore her with a lecture on the history of sports equipment, or opine on the incompetence of the bat boys. From the owner's perspective, these issues are irrelevant or someone else's problem.

Instead, I'd present the main context around the key decision. The owner would likely be interested in cost-effectiveness—which pieces of equipment, brands and models are best, the reasons for considering them better than the competition, and how much better we could expect the players to perform with them.

I would also be wise to build in a few extra minutes for discussion. People in leadership positions almost always request clarification (in rare cases because they enjoy seeing subordinates squirm, but usually because they value your perspective), so I could save the last ten minutes for Q&A, answer everything I could, and promise to get back to her on anything I couldn't. It would also be a good idea to end on schedule, for while speakers should always be respectful of their audience's time, it's smart to be extra mindful of the clock the further you go up any chain of command.

So think about your audience during message development, and tailor your talk to their likely interests, background and expectations. Kindergarteners like Sesame Street, grad students like equations, and leaders like meetings to end on time.

4 DOWNLOAD & UNPACK YOUR CORE MESSAGE

At this point you've clarified your goals, embraced your role as expert and teacher, considered your audience, and you're ready to add some serious meat to the skeleton you sketched in step one.

While you may be tempted to take what you have to the stage, every quality presentation I've ever given required reflection, reorganization and revision. I've thrown together shoddy presentations that got the job done. But every one would have been better if I'd taken the time to unpack, revise and reorganize.

This is because understanding improves when we download our ideas into some external medium where they can be clarified, polished and properly arranged. Think of it like math. We can do single-digit addition in our head. But multi-function algebra? Too many steps, even for Einstein. However, that same problem is easy when we write it down.

Say we've been asked to brief a fresh crop of congressional interns on Metro (subway) escalator etiquette. I'd begin by downloading my initial thoughts in bullet point form:

- ➲ The left side of the escalator is like the fast lane
- ➲ Standing in the fast lane will (understandably) irritate the locals
- ➲ When I first got to DC, I thought walking on an escalator was crazy, too, but within a week I was doing it like everyone else

The next step is to identify an organizing theme. No matter how complex the topic, you can condense it into a sentence. For example, "Good parenting requires love, patience, and a willingness to overlook your kid's mistakes, and forgive your own." Or, "Though Marx's account of the problems of capitalism is insightful, his solutions are neither morally required nor practically feasible." Or, "Public speakers require only two core traits: the courage to get up there and the commitment to get better." As a speaker, it's your job to figure out that one-sentence summary—a framework listeners can use to organize your message.

A draft core message for the Metro escalator etiquette presentation might be: *If you're going to stand on the escalator, please scoot to the right.* However, points that I failed to include in my original list that are coming to mind now include both the *why* behind the custom, and the qualifier not to take it personally if you get yelled at.

The Why: It's important to leave the left side of the escalator open for walking because a) many Metro riders have (what they consider) important events to attend, and getting there on time sometimes requires extreme measures, and b) many people use Metro to connect with Amtrak, MARC (Maryland's commuter rail system) and VRE (Virginia's commuter rail system) which run on tight schedules. Missing your connection can mean the difference between arriving on time or eight hours late.

You're Excused: People who work and live in DC realize that walking on the escalator is odd and are understanding when visitors inadvertently back up the flow. So don't take it personally if someone yells in your direction, asking folks to walk on the left. They're not taking it personally, either.

Now that we have a decent overview of our main points and the why behind them, we can move into full organization mode.

5 LOGICALLY ARRANGE YOUR IDEAS

When it comes to organizing your message, that cliché—*Tell them what you're going to tell them, tell them, and then tell them what you've told them*—is repeated because it works. Audiences better understand and remember ideas that are introduced early, clearly explained and then reinforced.

The basic structure that works for most any presentation is introduction, preview, body, recap and close. Depending on your subject, audience and occasion, you might add elaborations and clarifications, perhaps like this:

I.   **Introduction**: Hi, I'm [your name]—thanks for coming out.

II.   **Preview**: Today I'm going to teach you a bit about x, y and z.

III.   **Body**: x, y and z (include examples).

IV.   **Elaborations**: Extra stuff about x, y and z.

V.   **Clarifications**: You may think x and y are the same, but they're not—here's why.

VI. Recap: High points about x, y and z.

VII. Close: Thanks so much for your attention.

For the escalator etiquette presentation, we might arrange the ideas like this:

I.   Introduction: Hi, I'm Matt—thanks so much for coming out.

II.   Preview: Today I'm going to teach you a bit about Metro escalator etiquette in Washington DC.

III.   Body: Walk on the left and stand on the right. Whether you're transferring from the Metro to Amtrak at Union Station, or from the Red line to the Orange line at Metro Center—in all cases, walk on the left and stand on the right.

IV.   Elaborations: Just like on the highway, the right lane is for slower traffic and the left lane is for passing.

V.   Clarifications: This isn't expected in touristy spots like inside the Smithsonian Air and Space Museum, and if you forget and people yell at you, don't sweat it—they're just in a hurry.

VI.   Recap: Remember to walk on the left and stand on the right.

VII. Close: Thanks so much for your attention.

I begin most talks by introducing myself and thanking the audience for coming, and close by thanking them for their attention. The middle is pretty standard as well—I get the main idea on the table, explain it, elaborate, clarify, and reiterate. This template usually works, but not always.

For example, as a comedy club host, my routine would look like this: I'd welcome the audience, preview the touring comics, announce upcoming shows, plug the club's promo items (drink tumblers, t-shirts, whatever), deliver my five-minute joke set, introduce the feature act, thank the feature and introduce the headliner, thank the headliner and close the show with a raffle, a song, and an invitation to meet the comics in the lounge.

If I'd followed my standard model and previewed my jokes in the beginning—"Tonight I'll tell two jokes about parenting and three about teaching"—and recapped the high points at the end—"Don't forget that the punchline to my first joke was 'Unless you're Godzilla!' and the punchline to my last joke was 'Burn her house down!'"—they wouldn't have been nearly as funny. So use your judgment as to when diverging from the usual model makes sense.

If you'll be delivering an argumentative or persuasive presentation, you might explain your issue, preview your current view, support it with reasons, and preemptively respond to potential objections. If your material involves a historical account of a series of events, or future steps to be taken in a particular order, presenting your points chronologically will make them easier to follow.

For example, when presenting on the expansion of high school ethics bowls at a conference in Cincinnati, I projected a blank map of the US with the heading "Beginning of Time– 2003." (Ethics bowls are similar to traditional debates, except participants are not required to disagree, and are not assigned positions, but are invited to think through difficult moral and political issues using disinterested reason as their guide. Judged by a mix of ethics professors, public officials and thoughtful volunteers, the team with the most compelling argument wins.) When I clicked to the next slide, the heading changed to "2004," Utah turned green, and I explained how Professor Karen Mizell at Utah Valley University organized the very first high school bowl that year, basing it on the successful Intercollegiate Ethics Bowl's model.

With each new slide the date would change and different states would turn green—New Jersey, then North Carolina, Tennessee, New York, Florida, California, Maryland, Pennsylvania, Massachusetts. I went all the way up to the present day, offering details on the different bowls, and closed by projecting bowl growth in the next ten years, adding commentary on how I envisioned this changing America's (often petty) political culture for the better.

My point is that since the topic concerned a historical progression, the chronological ordering worked best. And the ever-greener map helped the audience understand how ethics bowls were growing, and how we might expect the growth to continue.

If your topic concerns a system of some sort, you can explain the whole then break down each part, or explain the parts and work up to the whole. Or you can jump into the middle and work your way out.

For example, if I were a nursing student asked to give a presentation on the human body, I'd begin by covering how the nervous system controls our muscles, how the digestive system enriches our blood with nutrients, and how the cardiovascular system delivers oxygen. However, a presenter could just as well begin with a blood cell and work her way out, or with the full body and work her way in.

You can also organize your topic according to conceptual complexity, or according to the importance of the ideas, or according to an order dictated by someone else. When it appears that different approaches would work equally well, go with whichever resonates with your personality and seems easiest to understand.

Last, though it can take some work, logically ordering your presentation has the added benefit of making it easier for you to remember. When your ideas naturally flow from one to the next, you won't have to put much effort into memorization beyond your opening section—everything falls into place.

For example, the first day in my on-site ethics classes goes something like this: After a warm welcome and mutual introductions, I'll explain that philosophy is the reason-based attempt to answer life's big non-empirical questions, which naturally leads to a discussion on differences between empirical and non-empirical questions, which naturally leads to a discussion on the nature of ethical questions, which naturally leads to an exploration of the differences between morality, psychology and legality, as well as refutation of moral relativism, which naturally leads to the alternative of moral objectivism, which naturally leads to the four dominant ethical theories, which we'll then naturally apply to particular ethical issues. (Don't worry, we revisit, unpack and analyze all this over the course of the semester—that's just the day one preview.)

You may not be versed in academic ethics. (If you'd like to be, check out my *Ethics in a Nutshell: The Philosopher's Approach to Morality in 100 Pages.*) But the point is that once we get rolling, remembering what comes next takes care of itself. Presenting is a matter of following where reason leads. And for audience retention, if a student can remember any one part of the class, he or she can figure out what came both before and after by asking why we were discussing that topic, and what we would have naturally discussed next.

Whether you're rallying a tee ball team, briefing congressional interns, or exploring the complexities of philosophical ethics, logically arranging your presentations will make them easier for your audience to understand, and easier for everyone to remember—including you. So take the time. It's well worth it.

6 BACKFILL WITH ANALOGIES, ILLUSTRATIVE EXAMPLES & STORIES

Once your main ideas are articulated and arranged, it's time to make them stick. My son better understood hockey when related to soccer, and you better understood DC escalator etiquette when related it to highway traffic, as well as the importance of stage time for new speakers when related to the importance of pool time for new swimmers. Such is the power of analogy.

When creating your own analogies, remember that they don't have to be fancy. In fact, straightforward comparisons are often best.

If asked to brief your office on the new computer security policy, rather than belaboring every detail, you could explain that it's like the old policy, except now everyone will have to insert their ID card into a special slot. Ta-da. If coaching first-time parents of toddlers, you could tell them that three-year-olds are just like newborns, except three-year-olds eat more, make a bigger mess, require constant monitoring, and will test your sanity at least twice every day. In both cases, simple, direct comparisons work well.

One of my favorite analogies uses the image of an elephant rider to teach the basics of motivational psychology.[2] The elephant rider, representing our rational side, is good at analyzing, setting goals and planning, but lacks the power to accomplish those goals. The elephant, representing to our emotional side, seeks instant gratification, and while powerful, is short-sighted and risk averse.

Without the elephant's power, the rider gets nowhere, regardless of the quality of his plans. Without the rider's guidance, the elephant charges recklessly toward reward and away from danger—he can't resist. But together they accomplish much, especially with a neatly-cut path to follow, the path representing whatever change a person wants to bring about.

The rider, elephant and path make the concepts more vivid, clear, and likely to stick in ways a technical explanation couldn't. Also, notice how learning about the elephant rider helped you better understand and appreciate the usefulness of

---

[2] The elephant rider analogy is from University of Virginia psychologist Jonathan Haidt, made famous by brothers Chip and Dan Heath in *Switch: How to Change When Change Is Hard.*

analogies. This speaks to the fact that concepts better resonate when illustrated with examples.

When teaching students how to write for clarity and concision, a fan of writing coach William Zinsser might cite both his good example of "Good writing is rewriting," and the made-up bad example of "When an authoring agent undertakes to commit thoughts to paper, he or she accomplishes greater success when writing the second time through in contrast with their first attempt at a written accomplishment." (In case you're reading quickly, clarification that this second sentence is an example of what *not* to do—more on Zinsser's principles in a moment.)

One pro tip from Carmine Gallo, author of *Talk Like TED*, is to make your examples emotionally potent, and when possible, to engage multiple senses (describing the look, sound, smell, feel). For example, rather than telling your audience that Disease X is responsible for a thousand deaths a day, tell them it kills the equivalent of two commercial airliners packed with passengers daily. You don't even have to describe the flames or screams—your audience's imagination will do that for you. And they'll judge your talk more compelling as a result. As Gallo explains it, "Jaw-dropping moments create what neuroscientists call an emotionally charged event, a heightened state of emotion that makes it more likely your audience will remember your message and act on it" (137).

You can also reinforce key points with callbacks— mentioning something later in a presentation that was introduced earlier. Comedians, politicians, songwriters, screenwriters, and authors use callbacks all the time. They're effective communication tools because they reactivate recently activated areas of the brain, which releases serotonin—a substance that we experience as pleasurable. Oh, I don't know if that's true. I'm a philosopher speaker dude, not a brain scientist. But one thing I can say with confidence is that callbacks boost audience receptivity.

I was honored to host my high school class's first reunion, and since I'd known everyone for at least two decades, could reference shared experiences that reinforced our intimacy— Ms. Lowe's obsession with owls, Coach Webb's constant need to tilt back his head to re-wet his contact lenses, and how everyone once thought Lillie was a witch. Not a mean person witch, but a caldron-brewing, spell-casting witch. Her husband, Dave, assured us this rumor was and remains false. Now the rumor is that Dave is a warlock.

You usually won't know your audience members well enough to reminisce your glory days or accuse them of witchcraft. But you will know them well enough to bring up points you made earlier in your talk. Highlighting that shared experience—even if it's a brief and superficial shared experience—will produce feelings of trust and warmth typically reserved for people we know well, and your audience will be more receptive as a result.

Callbacks also highlight your audience's learning. Remembering what you said earlier confirms that they're retaining your message, which is a boost to their view of you as an expert and teacher, and their view of themselves as a listener. For example, near the end of chapter one I mentioned that becoming an effective public speaker really only takes two traits: the courage to get up there and the determination to get better. As you may have noticed, I've reiterated that key point at least once since, and will reiterate it again before we're through. Hopefully this is helping you appreciate and remember the point, illuminating the fact that you're learning, and making you even more receptive to it.

Last, from fairy tales to religious allegories to date night at the theatre, humans spend their lives immersed in story. Stories help us make sense of our world, of where we've been and where we're going. Stories help us understand, judge and assimilate new information. And so it shouldn't be surprising that audiences appreciate speakers who storytell.

In *Talk Like TED* Gallo cites Princeton psychology professor Uri Hasson to make the case that packaging your message in story format also causes your audience members' brains to "sync up" with yours. Their thought patterns will mirror yours (or so say the scientists' functional MRI scans), and this "brain-to-brain coupling," as Dr. Hasson calls it, is ideal for idea transfer.

If you have little practice, start with *Once upon a time*, set the scene, describe a hero, a struggle, and work in a plot twist. Of course, make it relevant to the point at hand—don't recount your awesome hernia operation unless it helps reinforce an important idea. But do experiment, and without pressure to become a playwright. I'm not a storytelling master, but almost always use short stories to convey key points and entertain, and can confirm that audiences eat them up.

In summary, use analogies, simple comparisons, illustrative examples, callbacks and stories to make your ideas stick. Make them emotionally potent and engaging multiple senses when possible. Link your core message to stuff your audience already understands. And plant the suggestion that a random audience member dabbles in witchcraft for added fun.

7 Revise Using William Zinsser's Four Principles

In William Zinsser's now classic book, *On Writing Well*, you'll find four indispensable principles of effective communication. I keep them in mind anytime I'm writing or presenting, as well as anytime I'm teaching others to write or present. Those principles are:

Clarity: As Zinsser says, "If it isn't clear, you might as well not write it—you might as well stay in bed." Make certain your words convey exactly what you intend—no more, no less. The only time it's acceptable for an audience to wonder what it is you're trying to say is when your topic is confusion and you're giving an example.

Simplicity: Unnecessarily complex words and phrases put a barrier between you and your audience. Use simple, straightforward language, and refuse to indulge in pomposity. In fact, "refuse to indulge in pomposity" is itself a pompous phrase. How about "No fancy talk." No need to pretend to be smarter than you are with an inflated vocabulary. All it's likely to do is confuse.

Brevity: The human mind can only absorb so much at once, so make your ideas sharp and to the point. Concision is a virtue.

Humanity: Find, embrace and develop your unique voice. As I've always taught my college students, "Do not adopt the style of the philosophers we'll be reading. Even though they've authored some of the most amazing ideas in human history, communicating those ideas hasn't always been their strong suit." I liked this principle so much I made it a commandment. Zinsser and Deaton agree: Be Thyself.

Zinsser's advice is pure gold, and just as applicable to speaking as writing. If you burden your audience with a complicated, muddled message, they'll tune out. But give them a clear, brief message—and deliver it using your authentic voice—that's the stuff of quality communicators.

Zinsser also teaches that good writing is *re*writing. Babies may be born perfect, but ideas usually aren't. This is why revising your speaking notes and rehearsing your presentations is important. Each time through you'll think of new ways to improve—a more logical ordering here, a clearer example there. And while revision and practice take effort, if you expect your audience to give you their time and attention, respect them enough to deliver a polished product.

This is easier when you follow the advice of productivity guru Stever Robbins, author of *The Get-It-Done Guy's 9 Steps to Work Less and Do More*. As Stever explains, scientists recently confirmed what common sense already told us—that multitasking, while fun, isn't efficient, and tends to degrade quality. Although switching back and forth among lots of unrelated tasks keeps our brains stimulated, it also keeps them in first gear. But when we focus on a single task for a dedicated chunk of time, we acclimate, get in a groove and produce much better results.

Stever recommends categorizing the items on our to-do lists according to the sort of activities they entail, and tackling one group at a time. When it comes to public speaking, message creation and editing involve different parts of the brain. Therefore, when you're doing the initial "down dump," drafting the outline or backfilling with analogies, let the ideas flow. Don't stop to judge or analyze—just get it onto the page. Once you're through creating, *then* go back and change, rearrange and polish.

You can't expect your mind to create high-quality content when it's in edit mode or do high-quality editing when it's in create mode. So when you see an opportunity to do one activity while you're engaged in another, just insert a note and return to it later. Typing those notes in all caps will help you find them. For example, notes like DEVELOP STEVER TASK SEGREGATION ADVICE HERE and CUT THE CLUTTER IN THIS SECTION were strewn throughout draft versions of this book. The same is true for my presentation drafts, where I'll usually indicate my notes to self with brackets, such as [FIND A BETTER VISUAL FOR THIS] or [OPEN WITH SPEAKER SPONSORSHIP THANKS] or [CONFIRM PRONUNCIATION OF THIS DUDE'S NAME].

"Cut the clutter" is a nice bonus tip from Mr. Zinsser. Clutter refers to words and phrases that don't contribute new or essential meaning. Clutter confuses your core message and distracts your audience. Consider the following sentences:

1. I believe that cutting clutter is the absolute most important activity in which a person can engage when preparing a presentation outline.

2. When preparing your outline, it's important to cut the clutter.

Though both say essentially the same thing, the first is twenty-two words, while the second is ten. How'd we say the same thing with half the words? For starters, "I believe" is unnecessary, for of course I believe what I'm saying. Further, "activity in which a person can engage" is ridiculously cumbersome. Even the word "presentation" is clutter, for it's obvious from context that the only outline we'd be discussing is a presentation outline.

The second sentence is clearly superior. But it doesn't quite emphasize that cutting the clutter is *the* most important step, not simply *an* important step. An alternative, coming in at just under ten words: "When preparing your outline, clutter cutting is most important." Simple, clear, clutter-free.

Wall Street Journal columnist Peggy Noonan explained clutter cutting like this:

Remember the waterfront shack with the sign FRESH FISH SOLD HERE. Of course it's fresh, we're on the ocean. Of course it's for sale, we're not giving it away. Of course it's here, otherwise the sign would be someplace else. The final sign: FISH.

Clutter cutting can be painful. You'll realize that material you've spent hours developing is irrelevant, unclear, too long-winded, not true to your voice. And you'll be tempted to keep it.

Be strong! Keep and mold ideas directly linked to your presentation goals and junk the rest. And if you can't bring yourself to simply delete it, save your clutter in a second file entitled "SCRAPS." The SCRAPS file will make clutter easier to cut, and you'll have it should you change your mind or develop a similar presentation later.

Key Takeaways

⮑ **Clarify your goals and sketch an outline:** Begin with the end in mind—what you aim to achieve and your essential message

⮑ **Embrace your role as expert and teacher:** You're expected to understand your subject and transfer that understanding to your audience— internalize that responsibility now

⮑ **Consider your audience:** Tailor your message to match their background, expectations, and goals

⮑ **Download and unpack your core message:** Revisit and flesh out the skeleton you drafted in step one

⮑ **Logically arrange your ideas:** Chronologically, according to conceptual complexity, methodologically—whichever order will best facilitate communication

⮑ **Backfill with analogies, illustrative examples & stories:** Relate your message to things your audience already understands, and mix in a story or two

⮑ **Revise using Zinsser's four principles:** Revise everything for clarity, simplicity, brevity and humanity, remember that good writing is rewriting, and cut all inessential clutter

Chapter Four

COMMANDMENT II:
BE THYSELF

B eing your true self is an effortless, liberating, energizing experience. Too bad most of us don't do it often enough. We force a smile, suppress an accent, pretend to know or care about things we really don't. Before we know it, our sincere self is encrusted under years of grown-up pretend.

If you're old enough to remember Cheers, think of how great Norm, Cliff and Frasier felt when they could drop the pretense and just be themselves at the bar. Of course, they were alcoholics… so maybe they're not the best examples.

But reflect for a moment and I bet you can think of a certain place among certain people where you feel most in tune with your true self. A place where you don't feel the need to mimic the dress or attitude of anyone. A place where everybody knows your name, where they're always glad you came, where your troubles are all the same. A place where you can simply *do you.*[3]

If it's been a while since you've experienced that feeling, now's the time to recapture it. One of your goals as a person—not just as a speaker—should be to let your true self shine brighter and more often. (I hereby accept that goal with you.)

In a world saturated with fakery, people long for sincerity. So as a speaker, being yourself will be a welcome surprise, enabling an otherwise unattainable rapport. So let's give the people what they want, both on stage and off.

JEET KUNE DO YOU

The importance of being yourself applies to all you do as a speaker, not just delivery. Whether you're brainstorming, organizing, revising or rehearsing—do what works best for you.

This is the approach martial arts legend Bruce Lee used to develop his own system, Jeet Kune Do. Lee studied many styles under many masters, but never deferred to authority or tradition. Rather, he tested each posture, kick, combination,

---

[3] *Do You* is the title of Russell Simmons's book on the topic. If you could use a little extra encouragement, and especially if you're a Run DMC fan, check it out.

throw and submission for himself, and only internalized those that meshed with his body, strengths and natural style.

This is the approach I've used during my growth as a public speaker, and also as a public speaking coach. I've studied the experts, tested various presenting and coaching techniques, and only kept the best of the best. Continually learning, and with lots of room to grow, I'm always up for new ideas, but don't feel pressure to use every tip from every expert.

I'd like for you to adopt a similar mindset. The best way for *you* to prepare, practice and deliver, or conquer nervousness, or anything, depends on who you are. I therefore qualify everything I'm offering with the caveat that you should defer to firsthand testing and experience. Don't discount a technique without giving it a fair try. But if it doesn't resonate, don't force it. Your personal perspective and experience trump any expert's advice, including mine. I suspect Lee taught his students the same.

DISCOVERING YOUR STAGE SELF

As you work to discover and refine your authentic stage self, keep in mind that your "stage you" is simply one version of the sincere, full you. I'm a slightly different person when I'm wrestling with my kids, discussing bioethics with students, running a 5k, listening to a church sermon, or sparring at karate. This doesn't mean there's no real, authentic me underneath. It just means the real authentic me varies depending on what I happen to be doing. This is a good thing— we don't want kid-wrestling me discussing euthanasia or karate sparring me at church.

There's a public speaking me as well, which continually grows. I can remember dealing with nervousness in my first college speaking class by faking a huge grin during my first presentation. Apart from making it difficult to speak, my smile was confusing to the audience, for the topic was Oklahoma City Federal Building bomber Timothy McVeigh—not much to smile about.

As soon as I sat down I realized how silly I must have looked, how ineffective I'd been, and how terrible being fake felt. So I vowed to always speak with sobriety and sincerity—to be myself, whoever that self happened to be.

Over time I've developed a voice that's true to the real me, but tailored for the stage in light of my goals, strengths and personality. Anytime I catch myself trying to sound smarter, fancier, funnier, more interesting or more upbeat than I actually am, I try to remember that I'll be a much more effective presenter, and ultimately a much happier person, if I'm simply me. That doesn't mean I give myself permission to be grouchy on stage if I'm having a bad day. It means I'll coach myself into a better mood before I step up, which given how much I enjoy speaking, usually isn't difficult.

Discovering your public speaking self will come with practice, but you might begin by revisiting those times and places you've felt most like your true self—especially as a communicator. I happened to notice that I was articulate and felt confident anytime I welcomed a new person onto a team, whether it was a new kid at school, a new student in Jiu Jitsu class, or a new colleague at work. So now when I give presentations, I try to think of my audience members as new guys and gals I'm attempting to bring up to speed. The approachable, knowledgeable, avuncular personality that follows not only feels sincere, but captures a crowd's attention and opens their minds.

Before you can *do* you, you have to *find* you—or at least find your authentic stage self. Perhaps the best and only way is through experience and introspection. You won't know what feels right until you've been up there a few times, so if you're not presenting regularly, now's the time to begin.

Authentic Improvement

Last, being authentic doesn't mean you're locked into your upbringing or destined to repeat old habits, or that if you're not the same person at eighty that you were at eighteen you're a fake. (If you're the same person at eighty as you were at eighteen, something went terribly wrong.)

Being yourself means you are your own author, and that no one defines you but you. It means you take the initiative to think about the person you've been, the person you are, and the person you choose to become. It means that you're not satisfied to follow someone else's template, or to coast through life without pushing yourself to become more than you are. It means that you're committed to finding, embodying, and optimizing your true self, which changes over time. Authenticity and improvement are fully compatible.

Take a moment to reflect on your ideal public speaking self. What expression is on your face? How are you standing? How do you sound? What are you wearing? How are you interacting with your audience? What are you feeling inside?

Once you have that vision—a vision that's professional and polished, but unmistakably *you*—go ahead and *be* that speaker. Sometimes that's all it takes. We get locked into stories about how we're not good communicators, or how we're awkward in front of a crowd, and those self-limiting beliefs self-fulfill.

If you start telling yourself a better, happier, more successful story, it just might self-fulfill, too. If you can see how your ideal public speaking self moves, sounds, presents, and feels, you can become that successful speaking you. Give yourself permission to make it a reality. There's no good reason not to.

McKenna's Visualization Technique

If you're having trouble transforming in one giant leap, try doing it gradually with an exercise from Paul McKenna's *I Can Make You Confident*. McKenna asks us to imagine a slightly more assured version of ourselves—their posture, expression, mindset.

Once the image of your more confident self is clear, imagine them right in front of you, facing the same direction you're currently facing, with you looking at the back of your own (more confident) head. Now step (or float) into that better version of yourself, and change your posture, expression and mindset to match.

Now, having realized that slightly more confident version of yourself, imagine an even more confident you. What's different? Whatever the nuances, go ahead and step or float into that version. McKenna asks us to do this over and over until we're finally living, behaving and feeling like our maximally confident selves.

I'd like you to run the same drill, only rather than imagining a most confident you, visualize and realize your best speaking self, one mini-morph at a time.

How does your slightly better speaking self look? How does their voice sound? What's their attitude as they prepare and rehearse? What's different about their gestures, the way they walk, the way they feel about their message, their comfort with technology and visual aids?

Remember, you're only making small improvements with each morph. But once you've embodied the slightly better speaking you, imagine the next progression. Embody that version, then improve again.

If you can see it, you can be it. Sometimes it's just that easy. You can make incremental improvements with McKenna's technique, or flip a switch—whatever works.

The more speaking you do, the clearer your ideal speaking self will become, and the easier it will be to realize. As you push yourself to grow, remember that we're all works in progress. Being yourself is fully consistent with improving, and not just as a speaker. Feel free to imagine and realize your ideal family self, your ideal professional self, your ideal athletic self. With this one life, why settle?

The key is to improve in a direction that you rationally endorse and emotionally want. So think, feel, and become that ideal you. You deserve it.

Key Takeaways

➲ Audiences love **sincere** speakers

➲ Adopt what works for **you** and forget the rest

➲ Realizing your ideal self is **consistent** with authenticity

➲ If you can **see** it, you can **be** it—**give yourself permission**

Chapter Five

COMMANDMENT III: PRACTICE

Imagine Duke basketball coach Mike Krzyzewski studying film on an upcoming opponent, designing new plays to exploit their weaknesses, but never drilling those plays with his team. Imagine Coach K cancelling practice altogether, content that his Blue Devils are good enough. How well do you think those plays would work?

Before you answer, know that Duke always has amazing talent. If their blue-chip players happened to be facing an unranked opponent, an unprepared Duke team might still win. But against a good Michigan team? UCLA? Rival UNC?

The opposition would eat Duke's lunch, which I'm sure Coach K would admit. Those new plays they hadn't practiced, no matter how good on paper, would be clunky, leading to turnovers, blocked shots, and easy layups at the other end.

As speakers, the only real opponent we face is ourselves. But the importance of practice and rehearsal—even if you're as talented as a Duke Blue Devil—can't be overemphasized. That's why Commandment Three is Practice.

Practice is where everything comes together. It's where speakers go from shoddy to good and from good to great. And it's where you'll see the biggest returns on your time and effort.

PRIVATE VICTORY BEFORE PUBLIC VICTORY

The great Stephen Covey understood the importance of practice. He divided his 7 Habits of Highly Effective People into two categories: private and public, and his rule was that private victory always precedes public victory. Overnight, effortless successes are a myth.

Anytime you see a musician rocking a concert stage, an athlete winning a championship, or a happy, thriving family, that's the outward product of a whole lot of private work.

When most kids were playing video games, that guitarist was drilling new chords (and he has the calloused fingertips to prove it). When most fighters were hitting the snooze button, that fighter was hitting the heavy bag. And when most parents were vegging out in front of the tube, those parents were finding creative ways to help their daughter learn her multiplication tables, juggling their schedules to get her to ballet practice, and showing her by example what it means to be a loving, responsible family member.

Public speaking has "public" right there in the title. But the pre/private work—topic study, message preparation, rehearsal and continuous improvement—that's what makes our talks worth our audiences' while, and our craft something to be proud of. The beauty is that we can spend as much time and energy securing that private victory and setting ourselves up for the public victory to follow as we care to devote. But practice alone won't get us far. It has to be the right sort of practice, done in the right sort of way.

PERFECT PRACTICE MAKES PERFECT

There's an old martial arts adage: "The more you sweat in the gym, the less you'll bleed in the street." This may be embarrassingly macho, but the basic point is true. The more time and effort you devote to practicing a defensive skill, the better it will serve you should you need it.

However, dojo sweat alone isn't enough. It has to be dojo sweat excreted in the right way, the result of methodical, precise practice.

My old Silat instructor, Sifu Richard Clear, put it like this: "Practice doesn't make perfect. *Perfect* practice makes perfect."

The blocks, kicks, combinations (all the moves, really) have to be *just* right to work. While sloppy practice builds bad habits (as well as a false sense of security), focused practice, as close to perfection as you're humanly able, won't guarantee a flawless victory. But it will get you closer to the ideal.

As a martial artist, perfect practice not only requires using proper angles, balance and timing, but drilling as you intend to deliver: at full speed, against an uncooperative opponent. As a speaker, rehearsing as you intend to deliver not only requires projecting your voice, holding a confident posture and working through mistakes (you won't be able to call a time out and start over during the real thing, so shouldn't when rehearsing, either), but standing if you'll be standing, sitting if you'll be sitting, wearing a tie if you'll be wearing a tie, using a projector (or at least a TV) and a presentation remote if that's how you'll deliver. It requires simulating conditions as close to the real thing as you can get.

If you know how your audience will be seated (around a rectangular table, throughout an auditorium, in classroom desks), set up some chairs similarly and visualize the locale.

I've found that my kids' stuffed animals make for a lovely mock audience. They're supportive (especially Pooh Bear), quiet, and most even let me practice eye contact. I don't recommend rehearsing in front of unicorns at the office. But I have done dry runs in empty conference rooms—take my craft seriously, and know that the better I can simulate the venue during rehearsal, the better I'll be when it's showtime.

To add even more realism during at-home rehearsal, sometimes I'll have one of my kids read a prepared intro, I'll stand up from wherever I expect to be sitting relative to the stage, shake their hand, and begin. Yes, it's worth rehearsing simply walking to the stage, for nailing those first 60 seconds (and going in *knowing* you're going to nail those first 60 seconds) builds positive momentum like almost nothing else.

Bonus tip from a public speaking coach I can't remember (might have been a stand-up comedy coach)—if you'll get an official introduction, take the time to write it yourself. Email it to your introducer beforehand, and bring a printed copy. They'll appreciate the script, and you'll get exactly the set-up you want rather than something that's incorrect, distracting or flat.

For example, here's the intro I provided for a talk at a local philanthropic group luncheon.

"A Monroe County native and graduate of Vonore High School, Dr. Deaton holds a Ph.D. in social & political philosophy and applied ethics from the University of Tennessee. He's an Air Force veteran, author, keynote speaker, part-time professor and former Presidential Management Fellow. A husband and father of three, Dr. Deaton recently fulfilled a lifelong dream to become a competitive boxer and kickboxer which he recounts in his new book, *Year of the Fighter: Lessons from my Midlife Crisis Adventure.* Here today to enlighten and entertain us with some philosophical thought experiments, please join me in welcoming Dr. Matt Deaton."

The Sweetwater Kiwanis were local folks interested in local issues, so I played up the fact that I was a local, too—something I wouldn't have done for other audiences. I was also proud of my recent boxing/kickboxing adventure, so mentioned *Year of the Fighter.* And the thought experiments? Let's just say that linking drowning children to charitable giving and kidnap victims to abortion scenarios made for an awkward (though lively!) afternoon discussion.

Though they were a fun and friendly group, and the gentleman who introduced me expressed his heartfelt thanks for the scripted intro (made his job super easy), I got the impression they wouldn't be inviting an ethics professor to speak again anytime soon. At least not without pre-vetting the content. The lesson: provide your introducers a script, too. And don't ambush Kiwanis with abortion ethics discussions during lunch.

REHEARSAL REVISIONS

The first time you run through a new presentation you'll feel clunky and worry that you're going to bomb. Remind yourself that you're investing in your private victory for the public victory to follow, and that by the time you're done rehearsing, you'll look and feel much better.

At some point you'll have to accept your talk for what it is, and focus on getting so familiar with your material that you could deliver it without notes (no outline, no PowerPoint, and definitely no script). Once you get *that* comfortable, nervousness will decrease by at least half (if not more), and you'll be in a great position to enjoy your time on stage. You'll be gifting the audience the polished product you've thoughtfully prepared.

However, the first few times you rehearse you'll be tempted to pause and revise your content order, tweak your examples, swap out your visual aids. Give in to this temptation!

The first two or three times I rehearse a new talk is when my most impressive improvements happen. It's a matter of deleting material that doesn't fit ("cut the clutter" as William Zinsser says, or "kill your darlings," as Stephen King puts it), rearranging what's left into a more logical order, inserting a little levity or an emotionally potent example. I'll think of a current event or a local reference, a way to make the talk more about the audience, a nugget of relevant wisdom to share.

For some reason this stuff just doesn't come to mind while I'm preparing on paper (or the computer screen). But once I begin rehearsing, ah, improvement ideas abound.

I'll spend the first seven or so run-throughs making edits. They're heavier when I first begin. But everything is subject to revision. Then the last three to five rehearsals are for memorization only—no further (substantial) changes. I'm not trying to remember everything word-for-word. But I am forcing the material to gel so I can enjoy the benefits of Commandment I: Know Thy Material.

Your timetable will influence how late in the prep game you can continue to revise. But leave yourself at least half a day to rehearse the final product (a couple of days if possible). While it's OK to edit a written report up until the deadline, a presentation should be finalized with enough time to switch from content perfecter mode to superstar presenter mode.

GO ON SITE

So polish and improve as you rehearse (heavier edits in the beginning, lighter as time runs out), make your practice sessions as close to the real thing as you can (unicorns and teddy bears optional), and for really important stuff (only you can decide when this is worth the trouble), rehearse on site.

A couple of years ago I was invited to speak at a workforce planning conference in New York. I'd visited NYC to see the Statue of Liberty and Times Square, but that sole family day trip was the extent of my time in town. I think my Uber driver could tell and triple charged me (I now know better). But while I knew my material and had rehearsed at home, I was a bit out of my element. So I made a point to visit the conference location, and seeing it firsthand made all the difference.

While the fancy ballroom was intimidating at first, standing behind the lectern, visualizing the audience smiling, and practicing my talk made me much more comfortable. I felt a little silly doing this with one of the organizers arranging folders and nametags at a booth near the door. But I went to sleep that night confident that I'd kick butt when it was my turn the next day. And I did, largely because I'd given myself time to acclimate to the venue.

The threshold for a talk's importance to justify practicing on site has risen over the years. Stuff that used to warrant an on-site dress-rehearsal, I'm now cool practicing at home. And for some things, routine conference call meetings, for example, I can run through them right beforehand and do fine.

But don't underestimate the importance of practice. It's an official commandment for a reason, and the more seriously you take it, the faster you'll improve.

Key Takeaways

⮕ Rehearsal is when presentations (and speakers) go from **good** to **great**

⮕ Practice as you intend to **deliver**

⮕ Stuffed **unicorns** make for a **fabulous** mock audience

⮕ For important talks (or anytime you want to kick butt), rehearse **on site**

Part II

Developing

Stage Presence

Chapter Six

CONQUERING NERVOUSNESS

Every public speaker gets nervous. Even award-winning actors and seasoned news anchors get butterflies from time to time. I know I still do. Why?

It's a matter of confidence vs. stakes. When you're sure you'll do well and the stakes are low, you'll feel great. But when you're unsure, and when screwing up your talk might screw up your life, you'll be a wreck.

This is true for lots of stuff. As our perceived ability to perform goes up and the stakes go down, we're more at ease. As our perceived ability to perform goes down and the stakes go up, we're more anxious.

- ➲ Fully prepared & no biggie = **Confident**
- ➲ Unprepared & a big deal = **Nervous**

Consider two drivers caught in the same snowstorm. One's a native Alaskan taking a leisurely trip to the market. The other's a native Hawaiian seeing snow for the first time, rushing his pregnant wife to the hospital.

Obviously the Hawaiian is less prepared and has more on the line, so we should expect him to be an emotional mess in comparison to the Alaskan. But regardless of his mental state, the important question is: What should he do?

FOCUS WHERE IT MATTERS— ACT WHERE IT COUNTS

Beyond turning on his emergency flashers, concentrating and perhaps praying, there's not much the Hawaiian caught in the snowstorm *can* do. Fretting over what might go wrong (What if the gas line freezes? What if the road closes? What if the Abominable Snow Monster mistakes my car for a reindeer and eats it?) is worse than useless—it's harmful.

As Stephen Covey puts it (you can tell by now that I'm a Covey fan), the wise person aligns his or her "Circle of Concern" with his or her "Circle of Influence." Few things are more pointless than fixating on problems beyond our control. But few things are more useful than addressing things within our control.

Put another way, consider Reinhold Niebuhr's Serenity Prayer:

God, grant me the serenity to accept the things I cannot change, the courage to change the things I can, and the wisdom to know the difference.

We'll seldom be able to control whether our audience arrives enthused, energized and receptive, or depressed, tired, and... *blah*. We usually won't be able to control the stakes either, be it a grade for a class, a promotion at work, or the simple admiration of our audience.

So the first step in conquering nervousness is to direct your attention onto relevant stuff within your control, and to release worries about things beyond your control. In a phrase: *Focus where it Matters and Act where it Counts*. If an acronym would help: *FM-AC*. Just like a car isn't fully functioning unless it has an FM radio and AC (air conditioning), we aren't complete until we're Focusing where it Matters and Acting where it Counts. In both cases, the key is FM-AC. (Yes, this is corny. Yes, we're doing it anyway.)

Deciding to FM-AC ensures your focus is productive rather than destructive. And few things within your control can quell anxiety like knowing your material and rehearsing. Knowing your material and rehearsing... Where have we heard that before... Oh yea, Commandments I and III.

Fair warning that the drill that follows is slightly unorthodox. Ok, so it's very unorthodox. But I've seen it work wonders for new speakers, especially the shy and easily embarrassed. And it just might come in handy off stage, too, possibly near a library.

THE URBAN HONEY BADGER

In civilized society, physical intimidation is rarely overt. The pushy car salesman doesn't directly threaten to assault us if we don't accept his terms. But he may subtly suggest the possibility by standing up, putting his hands on the desk and leaning forward as he slides the sales contract our direction.

When we're sensitive to this sort of thing, we're more easily pushed around, more shy and less outspoken. Sometimes public speaking nervousness is the result of a physical insecurity of this sort. We're uncomfortable with confrontation generally, and while there's little risk our audience will attack us, related worries make us reluctant to expose ourselves.

One way to overcome this aversion is to learn a little self-defense. This is why I teach martial arts in my public speaking workshops. When speakers know they could at least put up a fight if forced, they're less reluctant to stand up for themselves, less worried about their audience's reaction, and less nervous.

I've used the Urban Honey Badger drill you're about to learn to help hundreds of students overcome longstanding speaking shyness.[4] If you've been passively reading so far, now's when I need you to become an active participant.

Imagine you're on a street corner at midnight, looking to score a deal on a new headset mic, when you notice a burly, sketchy-looking dude walking your way with a frown and menacing body language. Once it's clear that he's coming at you and not the vending machine beside you, you need to engage him both physically and verbally so he knows you see him, and that you're not afraid of confrontation. Turn to face him, bring up one hand into the "halt" position, and ask, "Can I help you?"

Go ahead—practice right now. Visualize the scenario, and take the initiative to confront this potential attacker with both a question and a hand gesture. He's probably a very nice person, hungry for one of those tasty Snickers to your left. But just in case he's an axe murderer, let's give him reason to reconsider his apparent choice in victims.

---

[4] The UHB draws on the teachings of three self-defense experts: Sigung Richard Clear of Clear's Silat (Silat is an Indonesian martial art known for its fluidity, viciousness, and use of weapons), a former undercover policeman who goes by SouthNarc, and Rich Dimitri, creator of a simple but devastating close-range technique called *the Shredder*.

You might *say*, "Can I help you?" but your body, your face, and the inflection in your voice should convey, "BOTHER SOMEONE ELSE." Your demeanor shouldn't be overly aggressive—you're not picking a fight. However, there should be no hint of accommodation. In fact, you might even lean or step toward him when you ask the question. Make it clear that while you're being pleasant for the moment, you're prepared to take it to the next level if forced.

If he never meant you any harm, he'll stop, answer your question, and be on his way. "Yeah, I was just looking for 1st Street. Know where it is?" But if he continues to approach, you need to elevate your assertiveness by transitioning from a question to a command, and from one physical barrier to two.

Firmly and with moderate volume say, "STOP" as you raise your second hand into the halt position. Whatever level of forcefulness you used in step one, double it. You need to make it painfully clear that you do not appreciate this person's aggression (whether intentional or not), and that you will not passively take whatever he's apparently giving. If "HOLD IT RIGHT THERE" feels more natural, that phrase works just as well.

If after asking your opening question, transitioning into a command, and clearly displaying the international sign for halt, this person *still* continues to approach, assume he intends to do you serious harm, and as loudly and as powerfully as you can yell, "GET BACK! GET BACK!" Show them your "war face," crouch down into a fighting/wrestling stance, and pump your hands with each syllable. Punctuate your commands with profanity if you're so inclined. This is no time for manners.

If the above sounds like the sort of thing you'd have trouble doing, you're not alone. Step three is where many students cower, cover their face, or break into laughter. But they're precisely the people who most need the practice. Assailants feast on timid victims, and pleading is unlikely to help, for if assailants were merciful, they wouldn't be assailants.

I actually used this technique to de-escalate a potential assault in a library parking lot, of all places. My wife and I were loading our kids into their car seats when I noticed two men approaching from the rear. I overheard a woman who was with them anxiously whisper, *"What are you doing?"* and my spider-sense kicked in. I threw up a halt hand and asked, "Can I help you?" in the firm way I describe above. The two men began to fan out, continued their approach, and the closest one asked if I had a light. I replied, "No, I do NOT have a light," maintaining the general "BOTHER SOMEONE ELSE" body language and tone. After only a few more steps, they slowed their approach, stopped, turned, and walked away.

Whether they really just wanted a light or something else, we'll never know. But the technique kept two potential threats from getting close enough to harm me or my family, and standing up to them felt great, at least once we were safely down the road and the adrenaline had worn off.

The technique also worked for a former student named Zach who was walking in front of the campus library when a man stopped him and asked for a light. (What's up with chain-smoking muggers at the library, I do not know.) When Zach kindly told him no, the man pressed forward, exclaiming, "Oh I think you DO have a light—*you DO have a light!*" Zach began pumping both hands and yelling, "GET BACK! GET BACK!" which startled the man, giving Zach a chance to run to safety. Maybe the guy just *really* needed a smoke. But more likely his request was a ruse.

In the first edition of this book, here's where you would have read: "The final portion of the Urban Honey Badger only happens if an assailant makes physical contact, and should only be employed when you're in reasonable fear of serious bodily injury or death. I'm not going to get that graphic here. Let's just say it involves mauling an assailant's soft targets in ultraviolent fashion—google 'Rich Dimitri Shredder' to learn more."

But since this is the new and improved edition, I'll go ahead and share a few details. Remember that this is for escaping a violent attack, not subduing rowdy uncles or winning playground fistfights. It's a last resort, used only when you have legit reason to think this person aims to seriously harm you. Play at your own risk, consult a self-defense attorney, etc.

Keeping your chin down, your elbows close to your body, and your hands in front of your face for protection, lunge into your assailant, latching your open hands onto their face like that spider thing from Alien. As you knee their groin, violently and with conviction gouge their eyes (dig your thumbs into the inside of their sockets and see if you can scoop them out), twist and tear their ears. Use your fingernails to claw and scratch and rip. Use the crown of your skull to break their jaw. Whatever of theirs is nearest your mouth (neck, digits, or my favorite, a juicy nipple) bite it off, spit it out, and come back for seconds. Feel free to add growling and mouth foaming for extra effect.

Keep in mind that while the initial goal was to keep the bad guy at a distance, you'll have to get up close and personal for this part to work. When physical confrontation is unavoidable (thanks to them, not you), it's time to go all in. Keeping them at arm's length and reaching for their face ("Hold still, I'm trying to scratch you...") would be easy for them to block, and would leave your own face vulnerable to strikes. But by crashing into them with your chin down, elbows anchored to your ribs, fingernails seeking flesh with bad intentions, you have a fighting chance.

If you execute with rage (channeling your "inner beast" as San Soo practitioners call it) your assailant should wind up bent over, face in palms, oozing bodily fluids. This is a good time to knee their face and run away.

Remember: this is only a last resort, and only for when you're in legitimate fear of serious bodily injury or death. Do not Urban Honey Badger census workers.

As you practice raising your hands and escalating your commands, get mean. Get loud. Get aggressive. Decide that you will NOT be a passive victim, and that anyone who tests you will regret it.

Find a place where no one will mind your yelling, and give those imaginary bad guys an earful *(GET BACK!)*. And if you have access to a "Bob" boxing dummy, go ahead and practice the close-quarters mauling stuff, too.

If you're finding it difficult to muster the enthusiasm to practice this with conviction, just imagine you're protecting a loved one. I once taught the Urban Honey Badger to a reluctant grandmother whom I could barely convince to stand up, let alone shout. But as soon as I threatened her grandbabies, she went crazy. Ms. Iris, I pray no one ever suffers your wrath!

Last, if this drill resonated (kinda fun, right?), sign up for a martial arts class. Experts argue over which style is most effective on the street, but studying any system is better than studying no system. One key is to switch from thinking of yourself as prey to thinking of yourself as a predator, at least when forced. Remember: you're an urban honey badger.

Cobras don't eat you. *You eat cobras.* Now take that honey badger swagger everywhere you go, including the stage.

THE MIND-BODY LOOP

Paul McKenna, the hypnotist who gave us the incremental improvement visualization exercise (where we imagine then step into slightly better versions of ourselves) explains that there's a two-way psycho-physiological connection between posture and mindset. The way we feel impacts our posture, and our posture impacts the way we feel. McKenna calls this the "mind-body loop."

While it's often difficult to simply *choose* to feel more confident and relaxed, we can indirectly accomplish the same goal by choosing to improve the way we carry ourselves. For example, think of a time when you felt self-confident and relaxed. Now, reflect on your posture. It most likely included shoulders back but loose, head up straight, belly in, chest out. Whatever your current posture, adjust it to adopt whatever traits you associate with confidence.

Notice anything? When we sit, stand and move as a more confident and relaxed version of ourselves sits, stands and moves, we actually become more confident and relaxed. We decide with our mind to adjust our body, and in turn our body adjusts our mind. That's the loop.

The good posture habit is worth doing all the time, not just when speaking. Depending on your current habits, it may feel awkward at first. But stick with it. Your muscles will strengthen and your ligaments will adjust, such that the upright, confident you will become the natural you, and you'll enjoy a happier and more positive psyche as a result.

So the next time you're feeling out of sorts (maybe because you had to Urban Honey Badger a library stalker's face), kickstart your recovery by improving your posture.

DRESS FOR SUCCESS

In the same way posture can impact our psyche, so too can the clothes we wear. Tony Alessandra suggests (and I agree) that it's worth your time and money to invest in an empowering wardrobe.

What that looks like depends on your personal style, and is likely to change. When I was in the military, I felt most comfortable in camouflage. When I was teaching fulltime, I felt most comfortable in a button-up shirt and slacks. After a few months in an office setting, I felt most comfortable in a suit and tie.

However, some people hate ties. If that's you, please don't wear one (use a pre-folded pocket square instead). And if you're not sure whether a tie (or pocket square) is right for you, an important presentation isn't the time to experiment. I suspect the same is true of high heels.

We'll talk more about what Alessandra calls your "silent message" and how you can mold it to suit your public speaking goals in the physical delivery chapter. For now the point is that you can temper nervousness by wearing clothes that make you feel good. But whatever you wear, don't wear it because it looks good on someone else. Wear it because it looks and feels good on you, and it's true to your authentic stage self.

And get a haircut. I always schedule a fresh cut a few days before a big presentation, and it always makes me feel better. My fifteen-year-old nephew is into perming his hair for some reason. So get yours trimmed, permed, braided like Snoop Dogg—whatever works for you.

RELEASE THE NEGATIVE & AMPLIFY THE POSITIVE

"I always mess up—I'll never be any good," my four-year-old said in disgust, walking off the soccer field after a frustrating practice. A teammate, only a year older, interrupted: "Don't say that. One time I said I wasn't any good at baseball. But I practiced and got better."

Now there's a leader in the making. To recognize that a defeatist mindset is irrational, and to have the goodwill and courage to coach a teammate—*at five?* Let's just say I made a point to tell his parents, and they had every reason to be proud.

Thanks to those words, my son's attitude changed almost overnight. He went from seeing himself as a soccer flunky who would never improve, to a rising star on a winding path to greatness, and his performance improved almost immediately.

Now 11, he still loves the game, and gets better every season. In fact, just this week while practicing in our back yard, he passed along that same advice to a neighbor boy who was lamenting about how he'd never be any good. "Don't say that. Tell yourself that you can do it, keep working, and it will eventually happen." When it comes to skill and performance, belief precedes greatness.

Take this common example: "I'm terrible with names." We've all heard someone say this—inevitably someone terrible with names. But as Susan RoAne explains in *How to Work a Room*, to begin remembering names, you must first stop repeating that you can't. Then all it takes is creative association.

Meeting a man named John? As you shake hands, look into his eyes and visualize him in the "john" shaving. Or imagine him reading a "Dear John" letter, or signing his John Hancock. Or combine all three: imagine John in the john, having just read a heartbreaking "Dear John" letter, consoling himself by signing his John Hancock on the walls. Creepy example, but try forgetting John's name after all that.

Meeting a group? Do the association trick for each person, secretly quiz yourself (so it's Sally, Fred, and crazy bathroom John), and confirm you have it right as you part ways. Should you forget someone's name, admit it, remind them of *your* name, and re-run the drill. The point is that anyone can learn to remember names. But not if you're stuck at "I'm terrible at remembering names."

Before you can realize your potential as a speaker, you must first believe it's possible. Try saying the following aloud:

I am an excellent public speaker.
I feel fantastic in front of a crowd.
I seek out and look forward to public speaking opportunities. And on stage, I dominate.

Don't be shy! This isn't something I made up. It's a Neuro Linguistic Programming exercise—powerful stuff.

Writing it down before bed is also a great idea. And it's OK to whisper or mouth the words if you're in public. But really, go ahead and say:

I am an *excellent* public speaker.
I feel *fantastic* in front of a crowd.
I seek out and *look forward* to public speaking opportunities. And on stage, I *dominate*.

If saying that feels a little silly, here's the mantra I repeated during my midlife crisis fighting adventure:

I am a battle beast... I love hardcore battle training. Exhaustion is simply a barrier to push through. My body will respond when I need it. I am more skilled, faster, and stronger than my opponent, and he will learn to respect me.

Fight training (especially fight training against bigger, stronger opponents) often sucked, and I didn't initially view myself as a fighter. I needed to step into the me I wanted to become (fearless, capable), and making that vision a reality was easier when I said and wrote the things that version of me could honestly say and write.

Spoiler: I didn't win the UFC. But I did hold my own against fighters half my age, and I had one heck of a fun time doing it, enjoying far more success than I would have without the benefit of self-coaching.

Often the only positive reinforcement we're going to get has to come from within. Not because no one else cares. But because everyone's busy with their own lives, and no one understands our challenges and dreams like we do.

Repeating affirmations helps bring the desired you into existence. You begin to accept that you really *are* a battle beast, that you really *do* love hardcore battle training—that you really are the badass public speaker you desire and envision.

It was Henry Ford who said, "Whether you think you can or think you can't—you're right." And it was my mother who told me, "Never run yourself down—there will always be someone else to do that for you." So whether you're thinking about your speaking abilities in general or a particular presentation, nurture your inner coach.

And when negativity creeps in, simply *let those thoughts go*. Recognize them for what they are—pointless distractions that are completely beneath you. Then let them pass on through your mind without further attention.

Remind yourself of past successes (in any area), visualize future successes, and accept that you're not here to simply survive on stage. You're here to dominate.

DECIDE TO DOMINATE

I once had a student named Tron Dareing. Tron-freaking-Dareing. What an awesome name. I imagined Tron rock climbing and completing secret agent missions on the weekends, which probably wasn't true... or healthy for the instructor-student relationship. But with that name, he had to be doing super cool stuff.

While Tron's presentations were always good, his third was outstanding. He was comfortable and confident, his silent message, timing and body language were natural, inviting and powerful, and he expertly conveyed his ideas with grace. Tron was a star that day. His presentation was considerably better than his previous two, and the best the class had seen in some time.

When I went to congratulate him after class, Tron smiled knowingly and said, "Since this was my last presentation, I decided to *dominate* it." Tron was a humble guy, and didn't say this in a cocky way. Rather, he exuded the satisfaction of someone who had accomplished a worthy goal.

Notice that Tron didn't "hope" or "want" to do well. He *decided* to *dominate.* This is insightful, for one of the most powerful things you can do is refuse to settle for less than your best.

Titling this book *Public Speaking for Ambitious Rookies* might have better captured the content. *Your New Public Speaking Coach* might have better highlighted the style. But committing early to *The Best Public Speaking Book* generated an optimism, drive and accountability that's been essential to its success. It's also generated a possibly unhealthy obsession... so consider committing to a *highly excellent* version of your public speaking self (more on how to avoid and overcome the curse of perfectionism in chapter fifteen). The point is to aim high, and to make a concrete decision to make your vision a reality.

When you act on your decision to dominate, this not only increases your likelihood of success, it decreases anxiety. As Dale Carnegie says in *How to Stop Worrying and Start Living*, "I find that fifty percent of my worry vanishes once I arrive at a clear, definite decision; and another forty percent usually vanishes once I start to carry out that decision."

So decide that you don't simply feel good in front of a crowd, but that you feel dominant. Don't simply hope that you'll become an acceptable public speaker. Decide that you're fan-freaking-tastic. Then do something to bring those goals about, for becoming your best public speaking self (or at least a highly excellent version of your public speaking self) is fully achievable. After all, you are reading and applying The *Best* Public Speaking Book.

BREATHE

One of the first things boxing coaches cover is how to breathe, the usual advice being to exhale with every punch. Why would an aspiring fighter need to be reminded do to something so simple? Because while throwing punches is a stress reliever, receiving punches is a stress builder. One way our body deals with that stress is by tensing up and constricting our breath.

This may have helped our ancestors elude saber-toothed tigers, but it's apt to make a boxer light-headed, slower, and easier to get knocked out.

Public speakers don't have to worry about uppercuts. But sometimes our bodies respond to speaking stress in the same way, tensing up and depriving our brains of precious oxygen. Realizing it's happening can make us even more tense, our brains even more oxygen-deprived. But the fix is easy.

Don't breathe so hard that your audience can hear you. But do deeply inhale and exhale at a relaxed pace, both while you're waiting to begin, and while you're speaking should you need a reset.

Doing this during natural breaks in your material is ideal. But feel free to pause anytime you feel the need. Don't explain or apologize. Just breathe. Then press forward. No sweat.

And speaking of breathing and sweating, nothing clears my head like a nice run. I'll almost always go for a jog the morning of any big presentation. It gets the blood flowing, releases stress, and I'll use the time to coach myself up and mentally review. Stretches where I'm jogging past cow pasture or crops, I'll even rehearse aloud, ensuring I have my intro, close and main points down pat. The cows haven't complained even once, though they have given me some strange looks.

FAKE IT 'TIL YOU MAKE IT

Aristotle taught that when you seek to possess a trait or virtue, you should act in every instance as if you already possess it. If you want to be more assertive at work, more loving at home, or more disciplined in your free time, beyond making the decision to bring about the change, act as if it's already happened, and soon it shall.

Imagine the speaker you desire to become, and in everything you do, *be* that person. In your preparation, your practice and your delivery, act as if your personal speaking vision is a reality, and it will be.

We can use this technique to promote success for specific presentations, and to even overcome nervousness. The phrase to remember: *Fake it 'til you make it.*

I've found that my own speaking nervousness tends to crescendo as a presentation approaches, but then almost always dissipates a couple of minutes in (often sooner). So long as I can get past the initial hump, I'm fine. And knowing that whatever anxiousness I'm feeling beforehand will disappear once I'm speaking makes enduring it easier.

One way to shrink that early nervousness hump is to outwardly appear as if you're confident and in control until your mind matches your body. This trick works on at least two levels. First, there's McKenna's mind-body loop. Confident speakers display confident posture, and when you physically behave as if you're comfortable and confident, your mind soon becomes comfortable and confident.

Second, there's an external speaker-audience loop. Whether or not you actually feel confident, if you can display the outward appearance of confidence, your audience will respond positively. They'll think, "Wow—anyone that sure of themselves must have something interesting to say." Their good vibes will work their way to the front of the room, and once you soak them in, your fake confidence will become genuine.

So remember: as your presentation approaches, regardless of what you're feeling inside, behave as if you're calm and in control. When you appear confident and relaxed, not only will this positively influence the mind-body loop, but your audience will look upon you more favorably, which you'll sense, and cause you to feel even better. Before you know it, your words will flow naturally, your audience will be attentive, those butterflies will disappear, and bam—you're kicking butt.

Take it from Aristotle. Speed that transition. Fake it 'til you make it.

IF NERVOUSNESS HAPPENS, JUST PUSH ON THROUGH

Sometimes despite FM-AC, despite knowing your material, despite developing the right mindset, despite the Urban Honey Badger, and despite faking it until you make it, nervousness still happens.

A few years ago, I suffered a serious case of sudden onset stage fright. My voice wavered, my hands shook, and an irrational panic grew no matter how hard I tried to reason it away. My nervousness transformed from mental to physical, much more than it had in years. And to make matters worse, I thought, "I can't get this nervous—I'm writing a public speaking book!"

A month later I got dry mouth on stage for the first time. I perceived the stakes to be high, and my comfort level was low. But my anxiety was compounded by the fact that I was presenting from a spot where a president had recently spoken. This was an honor. But also intimidating for a country boy from Tennessee.

The good news is that in both cases I was able to power on through. In the first, I caught myself worrying that the audience would notice my shaky hands or voice and think less of me. But of course, they couldn't. I've had dozens of students apologize for their obvious physical nervousness after a presentation. But hardly ever did anyone notice. Key lesson: Don't let the fear that others can tell you're nervous make it worse, because they probably can't.

In the second situation, I was more surprised than anything. "Why in the world is my mouth so dry? I bet Obama didn't get dry mouth. Maybe he would have had he known the author of The *Best* Public Speaking Book would soon be speaking from this spot..."

Luckily that presentation included a built-in break, which gave me a chance to jumpstart my salivation with some water. But even without it, I would have been fine. I simply slowed down, pronounced my words more methodically, and reminded myself that no one could tell my mouth was dry but me.

Remember that conquering nervousness doesn't always mean preventing it. Often the best we can do is minimize it. It tends to come in waves, which inevitably subside. So when it strikes, just power on through. Breathe, ensure you're holding a confident posture, and mentally regroup. The sensation will pass, you'll be fine, and no one but you will even notice.

ACTION CURES FEAR

Most of what you've learned here applies to nervousness that happens immediately before or during a presentation. However, anxiety can be just as disruptive weeks and even months before a talk. David Schwartz sums up how to overcome anticipatory anxiety in *The Magic of Thinking Big* with a single phrase: "Action cures fear."

A few years ago I volunteered to play in an alumni basketball game to benefit my old elementary and junior high schools. Since I had been an athletic underachiever in school, I let my competitiveness get the better of me, and came to see the game as a chance to prove that I was finally good at sports. But the game was also a risk. I could redeem my athleticism with a strong performance, or confirm that I *still* wasn't any good.

At first I felt completely unprepared. I could dribble and shoot, but not well. My left-handed layup was U-G-L-Y. And playing in front of a crowd? I'd never been good at that.

Rather than dwelling on how I rode the bench when I was a kid or worrying that I might botch my chance to shine, I got to work practicing ball handling, passing and shooting. I watched instructional videos, played pick-up games with friends, and drove my wife crazy dribbling in the house.

Schwartz was right. The more I practiced, the better I got. And the better I got, the better I felt.

By tip off my anxiety was completely gone, and I was simply eager to get out there and play. When I scored more points in one evening than I had in all my school games combined, it felt absolutely fantastic. Never mind that my left-handed layup was still ugly, or that I was trying *way* harder than anyone should in an alumni benefit game. (Dudes I fouled: sorry—got a little carried away.)

Practicing cured my anxiety about the alumni game. But what can speakers do to cure long-range presentation nervousness?

As soon as you know you'll be speaking, clarify your goals. Sketch the main points you'd like to convey, reflect on how to best order them, and draft a few illustrative examples. (Remember the initial "down dump" step from the Know Thy Material chapter?) Get that stuff out of your head and onto a post-it note or into an email to yourself. The idea is to take some control over the situation and shift from "I have no idea what I'll say!" mode into "With this much progress already, I'll be awesome come showtime."

If you're still feeling antsy, pinpoint the cause. Are you worried about a lack of clarity of purpose? About who might be in the audience? About how long you'll be expected to speak? Whether there will be other speakers? Whether you'll have access to a projector? All of the above?

A quick phone call, email or visit will answer the unknown and enable you to FM-AC. If the purpose of your presentation is unclear, clarify it. If you're unsure who will be in the audience, ask. If you're concerned about how long you'll be expected to speak, negotiate. If you don't know whether a projector will be available, find out, and bring your own if necessary.

In each case, isolate the issue, clarify the unknowns, and take immediate steps to overcome potential obstacles. You'll feel better as the presentation approaches, and do a better job when it arrives. Remember: Action cures fear.

Key Takeaways

➲ Replace worry with **action**

➲ **Self-coach** with that Neuro Linguistic stuff

➲ **Stand** up straight, wear **clothes** that make you feel good, and get a **perm**

➲ In all things, **FM-AC**

➲ Boost your **assertiveness** by practicing the Urban Honey Badger on the mailman

➲ When nervousness happens, **fake it 'til you make it** and **power on through**

Chapter Seven

INVOLVING YOUR
AUDIENCE

I cringe when speakers begin with, "Raise your right hand if you've ever [insert something trite]." While their heart is in the right place, that once useful technique has become cliché, and most audiences are not interested in playing the Hokey Pokey.

However, involving your audience is definitely a good idea. If done well, it wins their respect and holds their attention. But rather than pressuring them to extend their limbs on command, invite them to practice whatever it is you're teaching. When your audiences begin *doing* rather than simply *listening,* that's when idea transfer kicks into high gear.

BUILD IN TIME TO PRACTICE

If your topic lends itself to on-site application, apply it on-site. Remember, you're an expert and teacher. What better way to teach?

Often when I present on public speaking, I'll have the crowd pair off and give their partners a thirty-second talk on who they are, where they're from, and what they do for fun. Nothing fancy—just reflect for 2-3 minutes, write down a handful of bullet points, and deliver to your partner.

Once they're finished, I'll combine the groups of two into groups of four and repeat the process, each person taking a turn to stand and address their group. Then we'll expand to groups of eight, then to groups of sixteen.

By the time I'm ready for folks to come to the front and share their stories with the entire class, it's much less intimidating than if I'd asked them to do the same at the beginning. This gives those who've never spoken in public a positive first experience, and demonstrates how rehearsing boosts confidence and competence.

When I give presentations on self-defense, I usually explain the importance of awareness and avoidance, emphasize that the goal in a real assault is to escape to safety, and demonstrate a few techniques. But it's not until the audience is actively involved that they really begin to learn.

Whether it's sharing their own brushes with violence or practicing the Urban Honey Badger (by the way, that's a callback, and this callback to callbacks is a meta-callback), they learn more and have a better time when they're involved and doing rather than simply listening.

APPLY IT ON THE SPOT

A similar example: the last time I kicked off the schoolyear for my county's annual teacher in-service, I increased the likelihood that they would apply the message by giving them the time and tools to do so before leaving.

After establishing the importance of goal-setting and overviewing the elements of a quality goal (specific, measurable, attainable, relevant, time-bound—the SMART formula), I handed out pencils and paper, and asked them to write down the most important things they'd like their students to learn that year. These would become their personal teaching goals.

This wasn't an easy assignment for teachers used to following lesson plans set by the state, and some were more excited to do it than others. But it provided everyone the time and space to reflect, a luxury teachers often don't get.

Suddenly a passive talk became interactive, teachers felt more empowered than usual, and they left with a list of priorities to guide their school year—priorities they themselves had developed (rather than being dictated by legislators far removed from kids' actual needs). Find ways to make your own talks less theoretical and more immediately applicable, and you'll add more value to your audiences, too.

CONTROL THE PHYSICAL DYNAMICS

Speaker Alan Weiss *obsesses* over audience comfort. And proudly so. If it's too dark or too bright, too hot or too cold, if his mic is too loud or too quiet, he's not shy about making the changes necessary to ensure his crowd's physical needs are met.

From my experience, some things will simply be beyond your reasonable control. But the physical dynamics of your venue definitely matter, and one thing we can usually adjust is where people are sitting.

If you're in a smallish room with movable seats, consider arranging them in a V or semi-circle. This will feel less Brick-in-the-Wall-ish than the traditional columned setup. For even more intimacy, pull up a chair, sit down, fold your legs and begin. (The speaking experts who claim you can never put your hands in your pockets, never chew gum, never this, never that are full of it. Be thyself.) Demonstrating that you're relaxed enough to do this will encourage your audience to relax, too.

If it's a pretty day, go outside. My students at the University of Tennessee knew that nice weather meant moving class to a nearby amphitheater, and occasionally to the football stadium. Contemporary moral issue discussions are fun already, and even more fun when you're among nature, or at least more among nature than in a building. The only downside— passersby who tended to wear less clothing the nicer the weather. Philosophy is interesting. But it's hard to compete with 20-somethings' hormones.

As Scott Berkun explains in *Confessions of a Public Speaker*, crowd density also matters, for it's easier for audience members to tune out when they're thinly spread. But when they're close together, there's social pressure to pay attention. Plus, when seating's intimate, your enthusiasm (or intensity or disgust or whatever mood you might be trying to convey) can more easily jump from speaker to audience, and from attendee to attendee. This is also true of certain infectious diseases, so follow CDC guidance and adjust your plans according to the conditions on the ground... But this is especially important when you're telling jokes. If you can get one person to laugh, chances are better that they'll infect the people around them when they're in close proximity. Chances are also better that they'll infect the people around them with not only laughter, but the coronavirus... So again, make wise decisions.

So if you find yourself speaking to 30 people scattered throughout an auditorium that seats 300, kindly ask the folks in the back to move down front—problem solved. This will win you credibility points, and provide useful insights about your crowd. As Berkun puts it:

> "You spoke the truth about the uncomfortable nature of the room, and people will respect your honesty and willingness to take action to fix it. And for your sake, you've identified the leaders and the fans: they're the ones who got up first. These are the people most interested in you and what you have to say. If there any allies in the crowd— the people first to applaud or ask a question—you now know who they are" (49).

USE THOUGHT EXPERIMENTS

Whenever I present on political philosophy, it's obligatory to include the work of twentieth century American philosopher John Rawls. Rather than revealing Rawls's conclusions, I'll lay out his arguments and invite the audience to think them through for themselves.

Rawls was concerned by the fact that our personal perspective tends to shape our political views. Poor white males, on average, tend to favor policies that benefit poor white males. Rich black females, on average, tend to favor policies that benefit rich black females. Similar generalizations can be said of people of every socio-economic group.

Whether a person *thinks* their views are aligned with objective justice, unconscious biases often turn political reasoning into a game of promoting our narrow self-interests, with everyone trying to get the most for themselves. Earnest, enlightened political reasoning is therefore difficult, if not impossible.

But what if scientists could somehow alter our brains, causing us to temporarily forget our race, sex, income, intelligence, religious affiliation, hobbies, handicaps, passions and the like? Might that allow us to transcend our perspectives and think through political questions in an unbiased, objective way? If so, what sort of government and what sort of policies would we endorse?

Just as I put the question to my audiences, I'll put the question to you. If you didn't know if you were rich and famous or broke and homeless, Hindu, Christian or Agnostic, straight or gay, healthy or dying—anything about yourself that might cloud your judgment—how would you judge the justice of various public programs? If you didn't know your race, what would you think about non-discrimination laws? If you didn't know your gender, what would you think about sexual equality laws? If you didn't know if you owned a dozen guns or had never fired one in your life, what would you think about firearms laws?

Of course, I could explain how Rawls thinks citizens behind a "Veil of Ignorance" (blinded from knowing anything about their personal situations) would demand something similar to the United States Bill of Rights. Or how he thinks they would tolerate wealth inequality (even put it to good use by incentivizing citizens to delay gratification and work hard to our mutual benefit), but only if economic inequalities somehow benefitted the least well-off group (possibly by taxing the better-off to support education and medical care for the less well-off). Or I could present the common objection that Rawls is assuming people blocked from knowing anything about themselves would be risk averse (and therefore demand an adequate social safety net, in case it turned out they were homeless, starving, unable to afford life-saving medicines, etc.).

But by allowing the audience to run the thought experiment and come to their own conclusions, they're much more engaged, much more alert, and much more likely to come away with a deeper understanding and appreciation of Rawls's insights. Whether they agree with his conclusions is inconsequential. As a political philosopher (as opposed to a political activist), my job is to help people understand and evaluate arguments, not advocate for a particular point of view.

But my point is simply that when your topic is abstract, that doesn't prevent you from involving your audience.

Engage them mentally and/or physically, and they'll be much more likely to actively listen, and you'll be much more likely to transfer those cool ideas from your head into theirs. And if you can get them to sit more closely together, everyone should have a better time… assuming they don't spread a lethal disease and die.

Key Takeaways

➲ An **involved** audience is an attentive audience

➲ Have your crowd **practice** and **apply** your message

➲ Take charge of the **seating**

➲ **Thought experiments** help, too

➲ Philosophy is **cool**; the Hokey Pokey is **not**

Chapter Eight

HANDLING A
TOUGH CROWD

U sually occupied by hungry high schoolers, the cafeteria tables' round blue seats had been vacant since May. Today they were graced by the bottoms of every K-12 teacher in the county.

As I weaved my way into the crowd, I could see that most were attentive. Many were smiling. But one had her arms crossed, was tapping her foot, and gave me a "I do not care and go to hell" look that couldn't have been clearer had she flipped me the bird. Whatever her problem, when I paused to make eye contact, I caught the brunt of it.

Kicked out of my rhythm, I was confused. I'd put together a talk that was funny, flattering, engaging and concise. I'd opened with the fact that the group had just been recognized by the state as a top performing school system (as the director of schools had asked me to do). I'd spoken on how important the teacher's role is—how they're often surrogate parents—how many kids, if they're to hear an encouraging word or see a positive role model, they'll have to hear it from and see it in their teachers.

I'd included a few self-deprecating jokes about my midlife crisis kickboxing adventure (black eye and busted nose pictures included), as well as the story of how a student once threatened to burn my house down. From their expressions, most were having a good time. But not her.

Maybe she'd just found out she'd be teaching freshmen rather than 2nd graders (I'd be pissed, too). Maybe I looked like her ex-husband. Whatever the reasons, while I wanted her to enjoy my talk, I knew her problem was her problem. My job wasn't to make her (or anyone there) love me. It was to communicate the key ideas I had been entrusted to share.

Considering that this was a mandatory meeting that marked the end of summer vacation, I should have been grateful to see any smiles at all. Not even concert-goers are universally happy, and this work meeting in a cafeteria was far from a concert.

Just imagine the crowd at any paid event. Here are people who've traded their hard-earned money to see Lynyrd Skynyrd or Louis CK or Ice Cube. Yet there are always some who refuse to let on they're having a good time—won't dance or sing along, won't laugh, won't "steady mob" (Ice Cube will have to explain what steady mobbing entails).

Maybe they're realizing Skynyrd isn't as good without Ronnie, or that CK's jokes are just a tad *too* warped (on top of his off-stage creepiness), or that Mr. Cube is best enjoyed in the privacy of one's car. But whatever the reasons, no audience is ever 100% over-the-top thrilled, even when they've paid to see a specific performer.

Now compare those crowds with *our* usual audiences—colleagues stuck in a meeting, peers stuck in a classroom, relatives stuck at a funeral. Or (best case) strangers generally content to be at an event, but with little clue who we are, with little initial interest in what we have to say. Can we really expect these people to look and act like our biggest fans?

If you've prepared and rehearsed, taking the time to revise and improve before you deliver, your content and style will resonate with many, possibly most. But it's normal for some to be visibly unimpressed.

The good news is that public speaking isn't group seduction. As long as they're awake and generally looking your direction, they're probably tracking. (If they're not awake, that's when your assertiveness training empowers you to kindly request their attention.)

So let go of the natural desire to win your audience's approval. No performer is universally loved, and that's OK.

At the same time, expect to do well. Visualize success. *See* those attentive faces smiling back at you when you rehearse. But the reality is that not everyone is going to love you, and that's OK. It's even OK to bomb.

HIPSTER BOMB

I was once invited to do stand-up comedy at a variety show in an art studio. Figuring every speaking invite is a chance to grow, I agreed. I didn't expect to necessarily kill (after all, it was a variety show at an art studio), but I did expect people to laugh. I'd been getting better at open mic night at the club, and could hand pick my better jokes.

I began to suspect that my set, which focused on parenting, wasn't a good fit when the act preceding mine—an interpretive dance—went over well. (No offense to interpretive dance fans, but if that's your idea of entertainment, chances are low that we're a good comic-audience match.) When my opening joke about the host's husband's name (Levon) drew looks of shock rather than smiles, I knew I was in trouble. When I flirted with the idea of potty-training kids the same way I house-train puppies (*"Bad* baby. Poo poo outside—*poo poo outside,"* then rub their nose in it), my fears were confirmed: I was among hipsters!

My act was simultaneously too pedestrian and too risqué. They were appalled that I would suggest treating a child like a pet. Or maybe they were worried about the puppy... But whatever the case, what can I say? It was an art studio and these nice people actually liked interpretive dance.

About two thirds of the way through I noticed a red-faced gentleman trying to hold in his laughter. When he burst out giggling, I thought, "Yes—somebody gets it!" But it quickly became apparent that he wasn't laughing at my awesome act, but at how badly I was bombing.

This was embarrassing, and sucked, and nobody wanted to talk to me afterwards. I quietly snuck out the back during the next performance (a poem recital, as I recall). But the good news is that I survived and am laughing right now sharing the story with you.

It turns out that doing comedy at an art studio was definitely an opportunity to grow. I learned that bombing wouldn't kill me, and a hard lesson about tailoring my message to suit the crowd.

I also learned that it's a bad idea to make fun of your host's spouse's name. I wasn't a fan of *The Band* back then, but have since become one, and have much respect for anyone with parents cool enough to name them Levon. Special thanks to Ashley and Levon Addair—family friends and self-described hipsters—for that invaluable opportunity. Ashley actually designed the cover of my ethics book, and gives my oldest son art lessons, so we're cool.

A HECKLER? REALLY?

I didn't give up on comedy, and eventually got good enough to host at an actual club. In addition to welcoming the crowd, introducing the feature act and headliner, and telling your own jokes, hosts are expected to drum up additional business.

One spring evening the manager at Side Splitters asked me to promote a marijuana-themed show being planned for April 20th. For non-smokers, 4:20 is apparently the universal time stoners spark up, and April 20th, being 4/20 on the calendar, is a big deal for weed fans.

I mentioned the show during my opening, but didn't have any material built around it—just hinted at the fact that 4/20 is an important day for potheads, and that the club would offer an entire show of comedians telling nothing but weed-themed jokes. (The hipsters would have loved that one.)

Well, about ten feet from the stage there was a hostile-looking 30-something dude sitting with a lady friend. Maybe he'd had a bad day at work. Maybe they were arguing. Maybe his lady friend was the angry teacher from that school cafeteria talk. Whatever the cause, I could see from his face and posture that he wasn't in the best mood. When I mentioned the 4/20 show he decided it was a good time to interrupt: "Haha—*four-twenty*. Real funny."

If I hadn't been teaching college (teachers learn early how to deal with disruptive students), and not served as a security forces augmentee in the Air Force (guarding a gate with an M-16 and demanding identification from approaching drivers does wonders for your assertiveness), I might have been intimidated. But instead I paused, turned towards him, and said, "So you're a marijuana fan. Good—we've got a weed fan right here. Excellent. Hope to see you at the show."

That's what I said. But what I was thinking, which came through in my tone, was "Kiss my ass, dude. Let me get through these announcements, I'll tell a few jokes, and we can enjoy the show together."

It worked. Big Mouth shut up, my set went over well (much better than at the art studio), and soon enough I was introducing the traveling comics, having a good old time.

Hopefully you won't have to deal with people like this. But if you do, shut them down quickly, and make it clear that you're not afraid to engage. (Practicing the Urban Honey Badger will make this easier.)

One bonus tip is to invest in pepper spray! The kind they sell for bears works wonders on disruptive audience members.

Another is to deter interruptions by walking around the room before you begin, so attendees subconsciously know that for the next few minutes, this space belongs to you. You're essentially "marking your territory," in a friendly way, of course. Just don't get carried away and do anything the janitor will have to clean up.

WHAT TO DO?

If you get a foot-tapping, "go to Hades"-scowling teacher in your audience, bomb like me at an art studio, or some dude decides today's the day he's going to try heckling, just press on through. Some people aren't going to love you, and that's OK. Stick with the game plan, keep your composure, and reflect afterwards on how you can improve.

You can also try to fix things in the moment. For example, sometimes comedians will joke about how their jokes aren't hitting ("You're supposed to laugh now..."), and their willingness to acknowledge the obvious will win over the crowd.

A technique I've used to reset an audience that's zoning out is to invite a volunteer to the front to demonstrate a mixed martial arts technique. I'll get the volunteer first, then let the crowd decide whether we'll do a strike, takedown or submission. I'll demonstrate the move, have the volunteer do it on me, and usually that's enough. When it's not, I'll have everyone stand and try it with their neighbor (gently).

If that sounds like an exercise you'd enjoy leading, look up the basic 1-2-3 boxing combo (jab, cross, hook) on YouTube, as well as the "Osoto Gari" judo throw (one of the more effective and controllable takedowns), and the rear naked choke—*the* most effective submission, and it's not nearly as kinky as it sounds.

Or practice teaching the cha-cha, some yoga poses, whatever. Having a fun physical reset in your back pocket is a wonderful confidence boost, and it just might come in handy. Also, pepper spray.

If audience members are noisy or otherwise misbehaving, responsibility to correct them unfortunately falls on you. Usually showing that you're not afraid to call them out ("Sir, would you please hold your conversation volume to a minimum? Thank you") is enough. Just do it early (to prove that you will), and if all else fails, pepper spray.

Remember though not to be hostile or dismissive. We've all suffered through presentations where the most negative person in the room was the speaker. Be sincere and genuine, but strive to convey a collegial, inviting tone, even when people ask tough questions in aggressive ways. Your attitude is contagious, so steer it in a happy direction. As Brian Tracy puts it in *Speak to Win*, "The more low-key and friendly you are when you deal with the concerns or antagonisms of people in your meeting, the more open they will be to considering your ideas" (89).

Last, dinner talks are a special challenge because the crowd will be eating, half of them with their back to you. It's hard to compete with cheesecake, so ask everyone to continue enjoying their meal, but to turn their chairs in your direction for the awesome message you're about to share. Then ask for a round of applause for the kitchen staff, remind them to tip their server, and do your thing.

In most cases your audiences will behave marvelously and convey their appreciation for your message with their smiles, attention and applause. If you've put in the work on the front end, this really is what you should expect. On the off chance that you completely bomb, know that it'll make you a stronger presenter and person. And remember that a handful of unsatisfied customers is to be expected. Your job isn't to make your audience love you, it's to convey the ideas you've been entrusted to share.

Key Takeaways

⮩ **Not even Elvis's** fans were 100% over-the-top thrilled, so if your audience isn't gushing with joy, relax

⮩ Encourage respect by **"marking your territory"**

⮩ Engage hecklers **quickly and directly**—let them know you have the floor and won't be intimidated

⮩ Cheeky parenting jokes and art studios don't mix (though if you can **interpretive dance…**)

⮩ ***Bonus*** If in a formal setting someone asks a rude/overly critical/hostile question, **take the high road**—acknowledge their concern, promise to get back with them, and move on (their inappropriateness will be obvious, and so will your professionalism)

Part III

Mastering The Mechanics

Chapter Nine

PHYSICAL
DELIVERY

Consciously or not, people draw conclusions about our priorities, lifestyle, goals, intelligence and self-worth from to our dress, accessories, posture and mannerisms. We can ignore, lament or rebel against the fact that we're superficial creatures. But why not use it to our advantage instead? If you play the physical delivery game well, you can win your audience's respect and attention before you even open your mouth.

YOUR SILENT MESSAGE

I was introduced to the term "silent message" in Tony Alessandra's leadership and relationship development book,

Charisma: Seven Keys to Developing the Magnetism that Leads to Success. Alessandra does a wonderful job explaining the importance of sincerely listening to others, of having a clear vision, and of working with a team to achieve great things. But most important for our purposes are his insights on the power of image.

In an official speaking setting, a tie signals formality, jeans signal casualness, and a tattoo signals nonconformity. All three together signal confusion.

As a speaker, you might think it's always better to err on the conservative side and go with the suit or business blouse. But what's best for a particular occasion depends on the venue, the audience, your personal style and communication goals.

Imagine Farmer Brown arriving at the county fair for his cow-milking talk in a three-piece suit. In that context, wearing anything fancier than overalls (jeans and a Carhartt coat at most) sends the message that he just doesn't have a clue—about how messy milking a cow can be or the farming culture.

Philosophy professors at philosophy conferences hold a similar bias. While tweed jackets are acceptable, they assume anyone wearing a suit probably shouldn't be trusted. On the other hand, business professors at business conferences view anyone *not* wearing a suit to be untrustworthy—either a clueless rookie or a socialist spy.

The key is to wear clothes that are true to your personal style, but that at the same time promote your goals in the context of your audience's biases. Here's what I wrote about my own silent message when I was a graduate teaching associate coaching students on how they should dress for their presentations:

> I made a very conscious decision to stop wearing ties several semesters ago. Why? Because I was coming off as more stuffy and formal than I actually am. My students told me so. So I dropped that classic symbol of stiffness. I'm still rocking the slacks and dress shirts—just no ties. And that man purse I carry? A conscious decision as well. That's what separates students from teachers, didn't you know? Ever see a professor lugging around a backpack?

Having been an undergrad myself just a few months prior, I wanted to distinguish myself from the broader student body. If I had worn a t-shirt and flip flops, my students might have thought I was cool. But given my role, responsibilities and goals as a professor-in-training, it made sense to present myself as more of an authority than a peer. So out went the sneakers, and in came the dress shoes. Out went the backpack, in came the man purse.

Finding a style that felt right took time, and continues to change. At one time I was most comfortable speaking in a suit and tie. Then I went tieless for a while, adding a pocket square once I figured out how bland a suit can look without a little color. For my most recent presentation, I decided to wear a tie again. For my next, we'll see. Don't be afraid to update your own style as you grow as a speaker, a professional and a person.

Last, as we previewed above, posture also impacts our silent message. Have you ever heard political commentators say, "The president's posture was very aggressive in the last debate"? Or a sports analyst say, "That quarterback has to improve his posture if he's to lead the team"? The posture of the body under the clothes is just as important as the clothes themselves, possibly more important.

Slouching conveys a lack of confidence, exhaustion or laziness, and in some cases an acceptance of defeat. But a well-held spine conveys health, vigor and strength. And you already know about the impact of posture on the mind-body loop.

Whatever silent message you choose to present, remember that it should align with your immediate and long-term goals, and be true to your personal style. Playing this game is a little silly. But so long as humans are going to play it, we might as well play to win.

KNOW WHEN (NOT) TO LECTERN

"You should only deliver your presentation from behind a lectern when the microphone is bolted to it and you can't find a wrench."

I'm kidding now, but I used to teach this. My thinking was that a lectern (often incorrectly called a podium) serves as an unnecessary physical barrier, which tends to serve as an unnecessary psychological barrier, which undermines communication. I'd allow students to use one for their first presentation if they preferred, but by their second I expected them to walk away from it often. By their third I expected it to be used as nothing more than a base for their notes and water.

Dr. Carol Kinsey Goman argues in *The Silent Language of Leaders: How Body Language Can Help—or Hurt—How You Lead* that "a lectern not only covers up the majority of your body but also acts as a barrier between you and your audience," which is typically a bad thing when you want to connect and inspire. However, while lecterns do imply separation, sometimes that's useful. A president addressing the country, a CEO addressing her workforce, or even a principal addressing her school might benefit from sending the implicit message, "I have everything under control—ya'll can relax."

On the other hand, that same president, CEO or principal would benefit by going lecternless under different circumstances. Moving out from behind it conveys comfort and intimacy. It conveys warmth and an eagerness to collaborate. It also implies that you possess a confidence that doesn't require a shield.

I can recall one briefing in particular where a leader had just resigned, and his superior was brought in to reassure everyone that their programs and positions were secure. The speaker might have better conveyed warmth and compassion had he walked amongst the crowd as he spoke. But given that a disruptive change was underway, conveying strength and stability was more important, and his use of the full-bodied lectern helped communicate exactly that.

In that same assembly room only a few weeks later, the same audience reconvened to discuss a relocation of offsite employees to headquarters. This time a different speaker hardly used the lectern at all. Whether it was the result of her naturally warm personality or a conscious decision, she made it clear with both her words and her body language that she understood the audience's concerns about overcrowding and privacy, and would do everything within her power to make the move as smooth as possible. Taking questions, inviting the crowd to brainstorm for solutions, and giving every comment serious consideration added to her effectiveness. But her positioning amongst the audience most contributed to her implicit message of understanding and solidarity.

In the end, whether and when you should walk among the crowd or remain stationary behind a lectern depends on your style, audience and goals. Like much else in public speaking, the point is to understand the message that each option sends, and pick the best one in light of your goals.

EYE CONTACT

Eye contact conveys confidence, courage and warmth. It shows that you believe what you're saying and that you're interested in whether your audience accepts and understands it. A lack of eye contact suggests that the speaker has something to hide or is being deceptive.

So unless they're just too far away to see, or you're blinded by stage lights (which happens), make a point to look everyone in your audience in the eye at least once. The only exception: when an audience member has a face tattoo. For audience members with face tattoos the rule is *no eye contact—NO EYE CONTACT!*

This means you shouldn't bring a verbatim speech to the stage to read word-for-word. Unless you're using a teleprompter that's overlaying a camera lens, it's impossible for your eyes to be on a script and your audience at the same time. Instead, prepare well enough to be able to speak extemporaneously from an outline. Looking down from time to time to ensure you're on track is perfectly fine. Just rehearse and be familiar enough with your message so that you spend the vast majority of your presentation looking at your audience, not your notes. (More on using a script, on the rare occasion that doing so is appropriate, in chapter eleven.)

Also, be sure to spread your attention across your entire audience. If Grandma is sitting in the front row, make her feel special. But show the other attendees some love, too. Not only will the crowd appreciate it, having a speaker stare at you their entire presentation is creepy, even for Grandma.

If it makes you more comfortable, it's OK to look beyond your audience to imaginary people at the back of the room. You might think of a supportive friend (or me with my arm around the urban honey badger on the cover) smiling approvingly for an extra boost. (*You're doing great! We're not real!*) But do give looking your crowd in the eye a shot. The key is to keep your head up, address the entire audience, and look everyone in the eye at least once. At least everyone without a face tattoo.

USING VISUAL AIDS

While working in DC I had the pleasure of attending a leadership seminar put on by British author Paul McGee, author of the bestselling *S.U.M.O. (Shut Up, Move On): The Straight-Talking Guide to Creating and Enjoying a Brilliant Life.*

Paul proved a master of engaging his audience. He had us paired off doing exercises within the first two minutes, answering questions in our workbooks before first break, laughing and thinking the whole way through. Paul was also an expert at using visual aids.

Good visual aids artfully add to the show and highlight the speaker's key points. For example, Paul taught us four types of faulty thinking: Inner Critic, Broken Record, Martyr Syndrome, and Trivial Pursuits. I'll let you read the book to learn about the other three, but Inner Critic is that negative voice we're all so familiar with. It's a useless, destructive voice that tries to drag us down and beat us up.[5]

Rather than trying to describe it, Paul pulled out a big red boxing glove, and proceeded to punch himself in the face with it as he spoke. Brilliant! A memorable, emotionally-potent representation of the idea he was attempting to convey—that boxing glove brought the Inner Critic to life in ways mere words never could have.

Another visual aid Paul used was a rubber band. Anytime he talked about how leaders are stretched with competing obligations or pulled in different directions, out came the rubber band. He'd pull it tight, then stretch it a bit more, then a bit more, then a bit more—demonstrating the feeling

---

[5] Freud called that voice our death drive. Steven Pressfield calls it Resistance in *The War of Art*. I call it our bad wolf in *Year of the Fighter*.

everyone in the room had experienced, and highlighting the importance of taking time to relax.

Last was an aid Paul used in the very beginning and referenced throughout. It was a simple presentation slide displaying a one-week calendar, beginning with Monday and ending with Sunday. What made the slide impactful was that each day of the week represented a decade of our life. Paul had birth through age 10 beneath Monday, 11-20 beneath Tuesday, 21-30 beneath Wednesday, 31-40 beneath Thursday, 41-50 beneath Friday, 51-60 beneath Saturday, and 61-70 beneath Sunday. And when the clock strikes midnight on Sunday, that's it—earthly existence over.

Paul clarified that some of us are lucky enough to get holidays—another decade or two as an extra Monday or Tuesday. But through 70 is all we can reasonably expect.

I don't know about you, but I intend to enjoy an extra Wednesday! But the slide still generated the sense of urgency Paul was after. He wanted us to feel the need to act on our goals sooner rather than later, to stop delaying our dreams and begin realizing them as soon as possible. And he achieved that aim with that simple one-week visual. Somehow recognizing that I'm living the "Thursday of my life" (2nd Edition edit: I'm now living the Friday of my life—yikes!) made my mortality more vivid and my time much more precious than reflecting on a number. Thanks for the extra motivation, Paul!

Think of creative ways to incorporate visual aids into your own presentations. Use them intelligently, deliberately and sparingly. Remember that they should be aids, not distractions—they should add to and amplify the key points you're already making. Everything feeds back into that primary function of public speaking—communication.

Key Takeaways

➲ Improving your **posture** will not only boost your confidence—it will give your audience additional reason to pay attention

➲ Wear clothes consistent with your **personality** that promote your **goals**

➲ Use a lectern when you want to convey **formality**, authority, or separateness

➲ Walk around when you want to convey **warmth**, empathy, solidarity, or an eagerness to collaborate

➲ Use visual aids to hammer home **key** ideas

➲ Do not stare at **Mike Tyson**

Chapter Ten

ORAL DELIVERY

Oral delivery has four main components: accent, enunciation, volume and pace. Accent concerns the *flavor* of your voice, which should be true to who you are. Enunciation concerns how clearly you pronounce your words. Projection concerns how well your audience can hear you. Pace concerns how quickly or slowly your words come out, when and how often that speed varies, and your tactical use of silence.

However, don't be intimidated by the categories. So long as your audience can hear and understand you, you're good. As always, you're aiming to communicate, so don't get caught up in the science of resonance and refraction angles. Just speak up, be yourself, and focus on clear communication.

ACCENT

Part of what made JFK such a memorable, effective speaker was his New England accent. His words continue to impact those who hear them, not *in spite* of his accent, but in part *because* of his accent. Similarly, can you imagine, "I'll be back" or "California" without Arnold Schwarzenegger's distinct Austrian twang? His voice is an essential part of his multi-million-dollar persona, and I doubt he would have had the same success without it, glorious muscles or not.

I happen to be blessed with a mild Southern drawl. It's been tempered by time in the military, academia, and DC, but it most definitely remains. It's most noticeable when I pronounce any word with the "*eye*" sound, such as *hi, bye,* or pumpkin *pie.* So imagine how Southern I sound on Thanksgiving!

My accent occasionally draws notice. But given that I speak clearly and professionally, and the fact that it's a part of who I am, I haven't tried to change it, and have no plans to do so. I have the same advice for you.

If you're blessed with a Southern, Northern, East Coast, West Coast, Tex-Mex, Pacific Northwest, Canadian, British, Spanish, German, urban, rural or any other accent—go with it. So long as people can understand what you're saying, don't feel any pressure to change the way you talk, either as a public speaker or in private.

Your unique accent is just one component of your authentic stage self. It worked for JFK and Arnold. It can work for you.

ENUNCIATION

If you enunciate well already, feel free to skip this section. But if you're a natural mumbler like me, building your vocal precision is worth the trouble.

Enunciation drills abound online. A quick google will turn up at least a dozen, each set containing a creative phrase for every letter in the alphabet. Save your favorites and practice while in the shower, commuting, or right before bed. Pick two or three per session so you can focus on each unique sound. A couple I'll do before any big presentation are:

> "Rubber baby buggy bumpers, rubber baby buggy bumpers, rubber baby buggy bumpers…"

and

> "Queen Catherine *wakes* the cat and the cat *quietly* cries. Queen Catherine *wakes* the cat and the cat *quietly* cries."

The rubber baby and Queen Catherine drills cover a range of sounds, and the weirdness of the crying cat makes me smile.

I'll also rehearse my intro, paying close attention to the clarity and fullness of my voice.

Other speaking coaches recommend reciting poetry. So here's a powerful favorite by William Ernest Henley, his "Invictus."

> Out of the night that covers me,
> Black as the pit from pole to pole,
> I thank whatever gods may be
> For my unconquerable soul.
>
> In the fell clutch of circumstance
> I have not winced nor cried aloud.
> Under the bludgeonings of chance
> My head is bloody, but unbowed.
>
> Beyond this place of wrath and tears
> Looms but the horror of the shade,
> And yet the menace of the years
> Finds, and shall find, me unafraid.
>
> It matters not how strait the gate,
> How charged with punishments the scroll,
> I am the master of my fate,
> I am the captain of my soul.

I like Invictus. But if it's a little too intense for your tastes, here's "I Am The Ocean" by my talented aunt, Judy Overton.

I AM THE OCEAN.

WARM AND WELCOMING IN SOME AREAS,
COLD AND REJECTING IN OTHERS.

SOMETIMES APPROACHING ME IS CALM AND
SMOOTH,
OTHER TIMES IT'S COLD AND RUGGED.

MY WAVES EBB AND FLOW LIKE THE CURRENTS
OF MY LIFE.
RIDE MY CHOPPY WAVES HOLDING ON TIGHT.
OR EASILY BODY SURF OVER MY LAPPING ONES.

EVER CHANGING
BUT ALWAYS THE SAME.

I AM THE OCEAN.

I sense some suggestive undertones in my aunt's poem. ("Warm and welcoming in some areas"?? "Ride my choppy waves holding on tight"??) She denies any kinky intent, but you be the judge.

Whether you recite Invictus, my aunt's naughty poem or something else, pronounce the phrases slowly, overemphasizing each syllable, noticing how your face, mouth and vocal cords work together. The idea isn't that you should speak like this on stage, but that methodical practice will improve the clarity of your natural speech.

Another way to improve your enunciation is to listen to and repeat vocabulary-building audiobooks. While you may never use "soliloquy" in a real sentence, reciting it and its definition will help you pronounce the words you do use. The Princeton Review's *Word Smart: Building a More Educated Vocabulary* audio programs are great, but excellent free options are available (google "vocabulary audiobook"). And remember that just because you *know* fancy words doesn't mean you have to *use* them. (Notice how few fancy words I'm using here—our goal is to communicate, not intimidate.)

Finally, one easy way to improve your enunciation is reading aloud. (Consider reading the rest of this chapter aloud.) If you're a parent, kill several birds with one stone by reading to your kids. Few activities are more rewarding, especially if you pause to ask questions and discuss. You can't be Mr. Rogers all the time, but adopting his inquisitive, humble attitude definitely helps when reading to kids—check out the 2018 documentary, *Won't You Be My Neighbor?* for a reminder of his approach, as well as confirmation that he was not a retired CIA sniper.

If your children's library is bare, begin with *Where the Wild Things Are* and Dr. Seuss's *Oh, The Thinks You Can Think!*, two Deaton Family favorites. If you're not a parent, read to your pet. And if you don't have a pet, there's a Library Volunteer stretch assignment coming up soon (chapter thirteen is almost here!).

VOLUME

Professional coaches will tell you that the key to developing a voice that carries is to resonate each sound from your entire body. It should begin in your belly and flow up through your chest. You can work on resonance if you like (I do). However, simply matching your volume to the size and acoustics of the room will suffice for most talks.

One trick is to imagine lobbing your words to the audience members about three fourths of the way back. Visualize a streaming rainbow of words arching over those in the front and splashing on your target. But don't spit. This is only a visualization.

If you're serious about developing a full, rich speaking voice, find a copy of *Make Your Voice Heard* by Chuck Jones. Chapter eight, "The Daily Voice Workout" alone is worth the purchase price. Here's an excerpt that's not only enriched my voice, but cleared my sinuses.

"If you put two fingers right next to your nostrils, you will feel the flesh there is soft. That's the resonating area we're talking about… On different pitches, send the sound **Huh** out of your mouth (not through your nose). Put two fingers alongside each of your nostrils and massage the sinuses as you do different pitches… You won't feel a lot of vibration while you do this; you will mainly feel the pressure of your fingers. But after you finish you may hear more resonance coming from that area when you speak."

The sinus resonance drill is actually step 14 in a workout that begins by relaxing your neck, exercising your tongue, engaging your jaw and connecting your voice to your breath. Top shelf stuff. However, the payoff may be slow, so invest your time working your voice or something else as your circumstances dictate.

PACE

Your presentation pace should match your natural speaking pace. The only caveat is that you should speak slowly enough for your audience to keep up, but quickly enough to hold their attention. Don'ttalksofastthatyourwordsruntogether. But don't… speak… so… slowly… that… you… sound… like… a… car… toon… turtle. Find some comfortable middle ground that's natural and sounds good to your ears.

For extra effectiveness, adjust your pace depending on what you're saying. Slow down and lower your voice to add a touch of seriousness. Or speed up and raise your voice to indicate urgency or importance. "Please shut the door," can mean fifteen different things depending on how quickly it's said, which words are emphasized and how. Straining, "Please... shut... *the door*" suggests that if the door isn't shut soon, you may have an aneurism. Shouting, "SHUT THE DOOR!" suggests you *really* want it shut *now*. Use that flexibility to your advantage.

Last, remember that silence is your friend. The boisterous guests on television news shows have taught us that if our voice isn't filling the air with a constant stream of sound, someone will fill it for us. However, that's not a worry when we're delivering the typical presentation. The floor is ours—no one's waiting to interrupt. So use pauses to emphasize key points, or to plan your next steps.

In my typical Veterans Day presentation I'll talk about a local WWII hero's involvement in the D-Day invasion, a local Navy vet's service aboard an aircraft carrier, and a high school buddy's adventures in the Air Force. Audiences love hearing about themselves, and stories about local vets doing well connect them to a holiday being celebrated nationwide. But to ensure everyone remembers that military service is serious business, I'll close by honoring a hometown hero who was killed in action in Afghanistan.

I'll move through the comparatively happy military stories quickly and with a smile. But when I get to this young man's story, my tone is more solemn and my pace slower.

Sharing the details of his service, death and memorial here doesn't feel right. So I'll simply invite you to imagine how a speaker might use intentional pauses to give an audience a chance to reflect on the gravity of swearing to defend your nation from all enemies, foreign and domestic, and how in some cases the servicemember's oath requires making the ultimate sacrifice.

One last note on silence: if at any time you lose your place, don't panic, apologize or fill the gap with a string of "ums." (Unwarranted anxiety about dead air is a common cause of "ums.") Calmly reflect, consult your outline if necessary, and begin again.

As much experience as I have, and as much as I prepare, I still lose my place from time to time. In no case has it killed anyone. I once forgot the punchline to a set-ending joke at the comedy club. Sweating, blinded by the stage lights, sensing the anticipation of a couple hundred paying customers expecting a funny payoff to the setup story, that pause *felt* like it was going to kill me. But when I finally remembered the punch, the added suspense made the laughs that much harder—the audience thought the delay was just part of the act.

Your ability to calmly work through moments like these will confirm that you're in control, win credibility points with your audience, and boost your confidence. If you've prepared, your memory will eventually kick in. Trust it, and view those unplanned dramatic pauses as welcome breaks.

And if you're having trouble shaking the "ums," invite a friend to watch you rehearse, and have them yell, "Umm!" every time you say it. I've used this technique in my speaking workshops, and it can cure even the worst case of the ums fast. It makes the speaker painfully aware of when they're saying it, and gives them a powerful incentive to simply pause instead.

Key Takeaways

➲ JFK and Arnold used their accents as strengths; **so should you**

➲ If you're a natural mumbler (like me), practice tongue twisters or **read aloud**

➲ Speak **up** so your audience can hear you

➲ If you lose your place, calmly **consult** your notes and begin again

➲ Unplanned pauses give you a chance to regroup, and are **far preferable** to ums

Chapter Eleven

IF YOU MUST
USE A SCRIPT...

In their classic and definitive work, *The Art of Public Speaking*, Dale Carnegie and J. Berg Esenwein declare reading a scripted speech the lowest form of public address. If those masters considered scripts a bad thing (in fact, the worst thing), that's reason enough for me. But we don't have to defer to their authority.

Everyone knows scripted speeches are stuffy, usually only appropriate on formal occasions such as political rallies and funerals. But even then, a politician or eulogizer would appear more competent and sincere if speaking from memory, elaborating in the moment.

Your goal as a speaker should be to understand your material well enough to be able to explain it from the heart, using only an outline or a few notes. However, depending on your experience, I know the temptation to use a script can be strong. I used scripts in my first public speaking class in college, and read scripted lecture notes from PowerPoint slides when I first started teaching.

So while I join Carnegie and Esenwein in encouraging you to avoid them at all costs, there's no shame in using a script when you're first starting, if you must. Just commit to letting it go as soon as possible, and in the meantime, look up often and make sure it's written as you speak.

WRITE (AND REVISE) IT AS YOU SPEAK

For whatever reason, our written voice is a little different from our spoken voice. The way you would describe your weekend plans in an email isn't the same way you would describe them over the phone. Just open your Sent folder and read your most recent message aloud. Sounds a little awkward when spoken, doesn't it?

Reading a draft script out loud and revising it according to your natural speaking voice is therefore essential. Tweak any and all words, phrases, sentences and paragraphs according to how they best feel when spoken, regardless of how they appear on the page. Articulating exactly what to change isn't easy. But you'll know it when you hear it.

Be especially mindful of missed contractions. While you might write "it is" and "do not," you'd probably say "it's" and "don't."

EYE CONTACT REVISITED

It's hard for your eyes to focus on a script and your audience at the same time. But if you've rehearsed, you should be able to skim ahead, pause, and look up periodically. Please do. For added effect, look up at specific times to invite reflection on specific ideas. Journalist Bill Moyers did this well—look him up on YouTube for examples.

On the off chance that you'll be reading from a teleprompter (sometimes the boss or a producer will insist), at least you won't be looking down the whole time. It will feel awkward at first. But there's an easy way to get comfortable. Just google "teleprompter practice," paste your script into the tool, select a scroll speed, and read away.

Even if you're not using a teleprompter, the more you rehearse, the better you'll anticipate the sections and transitions, and the less you'll need the script. As that becomes the case, my advice and challenge is to trim the paragraphs into sentences, the sentences into phrases, and the phrases into bullet points until you're left with no more than a detailed outline to tuck into your pocket. If you need to use a full script the first few times you present, that's fine. But the goal is to go completely scriptless.

ABRACADABRA

I was still reading scripts in my mid-20s. But I helped my oldest son go scriptless for the first time when he was in the 5th grade.

He'd entered a school speaking contest and picked his favorite subject—Harry Potter—and written a two-minute speech on the Hogwarts houses. (Hogwarts is a wizarding school for kids, and "houses" are basically fraternities without the hazing.) We procrastinated working on it until the evening before (poor parenting, I know…), so I asked him to read it to me on our way to his Scouts meeting.

His main idea was that while every Potter fan wants the mindreading "sorting hat" to place them in Gryffindor (the house with Ron, Hermione, and Potter himself), all of the houses have their upside: members of Ravenclaw being known for their smarts, Hufflepuff for their loyalty, and even the dreaded Slytherin for their ambition.

Having read the book series at least twice, he was already an expert. And this being a simple two-minute talk, I convinced him he could deliver it with zero notes with a little practice.

He began rehearsing, and after each round we made it a little better. We added an opening to catch his audience's interest ("5th grade is when Hogwarts recruits get their admission letters, so if you get yours, don't worry you'll wind up in a house you hate"), and came up with a nice catch phrase: "Don't Fear the Hat." The more he rehearsed, the less he needed notes, until finally he was able to deliver the entire talk from memory. Believe it or not, he made that entire transition during the thirty-minute ride to Scouts.

He didn't win the competition, but came home with a beaming smile nonetheless. Why? He'd conquered his fear of speaking without a script, and now knew he could do it again.

You possess that same power. It's just a matter of revising as you rehearse until your ideas are so smooth that you can almost see the outline in your mind. (Logically arranging them helps.)

So write out a script for your next presentation if you must. But as you rehearse, my challenge is to trim that sucker until it disappears completely, like a Harry Potter magic trick.

Key Takeaways

➲ Script-reading is the **lowest** form of public speaking (Carnegie and Esenwein say so and Matt agrees)

➲ When you must, write a script as you **naturally** speak—using contractions, for example

➲ Push yourself to go scriptless—you'll appear more **competent and sincere,** and will achieve your potential faster

Chapter Twelve

USING
TECHNOLOGY

Whether it's a webcam, a microphone, a projector or a remote, the key to using technology is to become so comfortable that you forget it's there. That, plus testing it beforehand to ensure it will work and won't catch fire.

Anytime you have the opportunity, do a complete dry run on site, connecting all equipment to make sure it works. Confirm that the projector cables are compatible with your laptop, that the microphone won't screech with feedback when you walk to a certain area of the room, and that the screen-sharing web stream won't drop halfway through. These are all actual mishaps I could have avoided had I tested my tech beforehand.

It's best to test your it a day or two ahead of time so your subconscious can reinforce the familiarity while you're asleep, and to reassure your host that you know what you're doing and take your role (expert and teacher) seriously. But if all you can do is show up an hour early, that's better than nothing. Those few extra minutes have allowed me to track down extension cords, troubleshoot mic inputs—make all sorts of last-minute fixes that the audience didn't need to see.

USING A MICROPHONE

Mics take some getting used to. If it's wired, one of your hands will be constantly occupied, and you'll have to watch for the cord to avoid tripping. One tip I learned from the comedy pros about using a wired mic is to avoid the temptation to wrap excess cord around your hand. Doing so distracts both you and the audience, so just let that cord lie.

If it's a stationary lectern mic, you won't be able to walk around as you might otherwise prefer. Even if it's wireless, you'll have to carry around this extra "thing" while you deliver. So if you're not used to using one, it's important to rehearse as you plan to deliver.

Practice on site if you can. But if you can't and you know that you'll be anchored to a lectern, turn a cardboard box upside down on a table, stab a pencil in the top, and pretend it's your grand stage. If you know you'll be using a corded mic, practice with a hairdryer. A wireless mic, a magic marker. Just don't do any of this in public.

A couple of years ago I invested in a nice flesh-toned headset mic, transmitter and receiver—the kind tech company CEOs and TED Talkers use. It's my favorite mic by far, but often trying to integrate it with a venue's existing audio equipment makes the audio-visual people nervous, and adds an unnecessary layer of complexity. It did however once save a presentation at a middle school. The gymnasium was packed, I'd already delivered my portion, and when the school's mic failed, I was able to offer my headset and save the day.

If your host outfits you with one of those or a lapel mic, consider yourself lucky. Comfortable and sensitive, your hands will be free to do whatever they naturally do. Just remember that anytime you're mic'ed up, it could be hot, so no Billy Bush locker room talk.

THE JOYS OF POWERPOINT

The key to effectively using presentation software such as PowerPoint, Keynote (Mac only), Impress (free), GoogleDocs (free), and Prezi (cool, but dizzying, so use with caution) is remembering that it's an aid, not a crutch or a replacement. You and your slides should work together symbiotically, with whatever's on the screen complementing your delivery rather than stealing the show.

This wasn't always the case, but today I actually feel better with PowerPoint than without it. It helps me organize my ideas during prep, ensures I never get too far off track during delivery, and elevates the professional feel. However, a shoddy slide show poorly integrated (or used as a replacement for a real speaker) can make an otherwise polished speaker look tacky.

One way to ensure the software adds rather than takes away from your effectiveness is to use visualizations to illustrate and amplify your ideas. At the same time, if your slides could replace you, you're using too many and/or too much text, and your audience might be better off reading a written report instead.

So PowerPoint tip #1: Don't put every detail in your "slide deck," as they call it in DC. The key information should come from you, not the screen. The slides are there to reiterate, punctuate, illuminate. But you're still the main show.

The rule of thumb is that fewer slides are better than more slides and pictures trump text. Googling key terms and clicking "Images" is an easy way to find relevant visuals. (If you're paranoid about copyright law, clear it with the creator, contact an attorney, or spend a little at a stock photo site.)

Go easy on the text. PowerPoint should add to and reinforce what you're saying, not repeat it verbatim. Keep your bullets to phrases or short sentence fragments, and use them just as you would an outline—not as a script.

That said, some organizations will expect (even demand) that everything you cover be written out on your slides. This can be frustrating—like insisting Picasso use crayons or Pavarotti a kazoo. But if the boss insists, the boss insists. My compromise is to use as little text and as many images as I can get away with. And when I'm in complete control, that usually means zero text. Well, maybe a catch phrase or two, like Commit Begin Research (my success simplified formula, which happens to share an acronym with Honda's sportiest crotch rocket, their CBR), or Scary Authentic Proud (my criteria for planning life-affirming adventures, with an appropriate acronym since it's a little sappy) or Focus where it Matters and Act where it Counts (you know that one). But otherwise, very little text, and the right number of relevant, striking images.

Second, when it comes to animation, skip the text that spins or glows, or slides that transition by swirling off the screen. When I click my remote, I want the new slide to simply replace the old, and for the bullets (when I'm using bullets—prefer images) to simply appear. More than that looks gimmicky. However, if spinning text fits the topic (airplane propellers, ice skaters, tornadoes?) or who you are (a Whirling Dervish?), by all means, spin away.

One visual effect that I have had some success with is brief video clips. During a recent Veterans Day program, I used a fifteen-second clip of an F-22 Raptor doing a combat takeoff to illustrate a local vet's service in Alaska. In a hurry to greet Russian bombers flirting with our border, our pilots would begin their takeoff per usual, but once off the ground kick in the Raptors' afterburners and shoot straight up—an awesome sight for Airman Moore to see in person, and a vivid surprise for my Vets Day audience.

During a recent motivational talk I used a twenty-second clip from my midlife crisis kickboxing bout to illustrate the importance of self-coaching. On the verge of getting knocked out by a Superman punch from a shaved-headed, tattooed fighter half my age, I had to decide whether to listen to my bad wolf and give up (surprisingly tempting, succumbing to the knockout meant I could finally rest, and avoid additional Superman punches to the face) or my good wolf and fight back.

I won't spoil the outcome, but my point here is that a brief vid strategically placed can be a crowd-pleaser. Just download or convert your clip into MP4 format, paste it into a slide, and right click to choose whether it will begin playing as soon as the slide appears or on the next click. If the tech screws up (mine did that day, beginning my kickboxing match as soon as it appeared rather than waiting for another click), just roll with it. I had to tweak some points I'd planned to deliver before the clip on the fly. But my audience had no idea anything was awry—neither will yours.

Third, have I mentioned the importance of knowing your material? A fast way to kill your credibility is to look at each new slide before speaking, as if you need a reminder of what you're supposed to be talking about. An even faster way is to read the slide. The PowerPoint Failure Formula: click, look, read. "This slide is saying" (then read something everyone can plainly see).

Knowing your material means being fully aware of your slide order from beginning to end. It means knowing what's about to appear before you hit that clicker (and not because you can see the preview on your laptop).

A good way to test whether you know your slides well enough is to rehearse without them. I'll do this during my morning run, in the shower getting ready, or in the car on the way to a talk. Not only does this make me much smoother during delivery, it's also reassuring. I know that even if the projector dies, my presentation won't.

That level of familiarity allows me to look my audience in the eye, allude to the next slide, hit the clicker, *know* what's now on the screen behind me, and continue without looking back. Not quite as cool as an action hero nonchalantly walking from an explosion. But close. You can be Vin Diesel with a clicker, too. Just a matter of practicing.

Last, invest in a quality remote to run your slides from afar. Having used one for years, I can't imagine returning to the computer to fumble with the keyboard every transition. Even having to tell an operator, "Next slide, please" would disrupt my flow.

While my latest clicker upgrade includes a vibrating timer, I've only used that feature once. The basic models will do—just need the slides to reliably transition when you click, which means getting one with good range. No need for a laser pointer unless you'll be briefing at the Pentagon.[6]

VIRTUAL REHEARSAL

In chapter five I confessed to using stuffed animals to simulate an audience during rehearsal. I actually enjoy talking to unicorns (and they enjoy hearing me). But there are also some cool apps made specifically for public speakers that will immerse you in 360-degree virtual reality audience glory.

"Beyond VR" will let you rehearse in a boardroom, a classroom, an auditorium. The audience members squirm, nod their heads, scratch their shoulders. You can even simulate a

---

[6] My current clicker, inspired by Scott Berkun's enthusiasm for a similar model in *Confessions of a Public Speaker*, is a Logitech R800, ~$50 at Amazon. But I still carry and sometimes use old faithful, a Kensington 33373, which was closer to 30 bucks.

job interview. Select the tech version and one of the dudes asking questions is Elon-freaking-Musk.

It's eerily realistic, and could really help a person without much experience, especially if they were fresh out of stuffed animals and willing to spend $20 on a VR headset for their phone. If that's you, check it out.

PRESENTING REMOTELY

Whether it's via Zoom, Citrix, YouTube Live or good old teleconference, the challenge of holding a remote audience's attention increases tenfold. It's tough enough for people to resist checking their phones when they're sitting right in front of you. Imagine the multitasking when they're out of sight.

You'll therefore have to up your audience engagement game, but your job as remote presenter is actually easier in many ways. If it's audio only, you won't have to worry about your silent message (though you won't be able to use it to your advantage, either). And while you should still prepare a clear presentation and rehearse, you won't need to master your material *quite* as well as if you were delivering it in person—can always pull up reference materials, refer back to your notes, and have a timer in front of you to ensure you stay on schedule (though definitely still rehearse, still know what material is coming before it arrives).

This past January, I was honored to be invited to discuss my *Ethics in a Nutshell: The Philosopher's Approach to Morality in 100 Pages* with Chinese Ethics Bowl students. Thanks to tensions over Taiwan, economic competitiveness and the coronavirus (dang, China, you really screwed the pooch on that one), our governments aren't the closest allies. Many consider an eventual Sino-American war inevitable. So I viewed the session as an opportunity to befriend ethics-minded future leaders, and maybe, in some small way, decrease the chances that my grandkids will be fighting China in World War III.

I asked the host if there was anything I might do or say to express my goodwill and respect, and he suggested a line from a famous Chinese poem. So my first words were, "Sheeyan chew woo yuan tchin, wa leeee, shan weigh lin." Given my Tennessee drawl and the fact that I know zero Mandarin, I'm certain I butchered this badly. But it was supposed to roughly translate, "People can become friends and neighbors, even when they're on the other side of the world." The attendees seemed to appreciate the effort, and I very much enjoyed discussing argument by analogy, why we can't base morality on legality, and other cool ideas with them. You can actually watch it yourself. Just search YouTube for "Deaton Ethics Bowl China Seminar."

A couple of months after that, I was asked to kickoff a series of trainings for Ethics Olympiad participants in Australia.

Another chance for cultural exchange, I opened by pulling out a globe. "If you were to get on a plane and fly all the way across the Pacific Ocean and land on the West Coast of the US, then drive east for 3-to-4 days, you'd make your way to the foothills of the Appalachian Mountains in the great state of Tennessee, which is where I live. What do Tennesseans do for fun? Well, lots of things, but in addition to soccer and ATV-riding, my own family enjoys trips to the mountains. Here's a picture of us swimming at Indian Boundary Lake in the Cherokee National Forest." About that time, I (and everyone else) heard a young man who'd forgotten to mute his mic say, "No, he's still talking about his stupid family…" *Ha!* The Zoom screen was filled with faces, and from the look on his, he really wanted to blend in with the crowd. But since his mic was hot, his box lit up, I stopped, squinted to read his name, and immediately called him out. "Mickey Boffsetter? My *stupid* family? Did you not hear the host explain that I'm a kickboxer?" I rolled my chair backwards to the desk behind me and retrieved my "Fight of the Night" boxing trophy. "Do you see this? Don't make me come to Australia."

I was of course smiling and kidding, and he was of course *mortified*—tried to apologize and make excuses. "Sir, what I meant was…" But I just cut him off and poured it on thicker, which the audience loved—they were rolling with surprised laughter.

Another remote meeting icebreaker example, I once led a series of online workshops for offices interested in improving communication. Some had interpersonal issues (aka they hated each other), so I chose a lighthearted opener: Name That Tune. The first song: a Janet Jackson B-side track from 1984, "Communication." Some recognized her voice, but no one got the song. The second was Led Zeppelin's "Communication Breakdown," which a few middle-aged white dudes knew. And the last was The Beastie Boys' "Sure Shot" from their *Ill Communication* album, which no one but me admitted to ever hearing, let alone liking.

By the end most of the attendees were at least grinning, everyone knew the session's focus would be improving communication, and that I was an approachable host with excellent musical taste.

Another example: I once gave a webinar on business ethics to a mixed group of human resource specialists, website designers and managers. To get them in the ethical thinking mood, I began with what philosophers, attorneys and fans of NBC's "The Good Place" know as the classic trolley scenario.

Imagine seeing a runaway trolley about to crash into and kill five track workers. You then notice that you're standing next to a lever that can divert the trolley onto another track, sparing the first five, but killing another worker. What should you do?

Stand by and allow the original five to die? Or pull the lever, save the five, but effectively kill the one?

I then asked an open-ended question. "What do you think a person in this situation should do, *and why?*" This led to a conversation on the differences between psychological predictability, legal permissibility, and moral rightness, and opened the participants' minds in ways a poll or monologue never could have. When we got to the case study on employee privacy, I had no trouble getting folks to discuss, which was my goal all along.

In cases of remote audience disengagement emergency, one somewhat mean tactic is to ask a question and call on attendees by name (depending on the software, you should be able to see their names right there on the screen). Once you've called on a couple, everyone will pay attention so they don't get caught dozing. But again, this is mean, so if you do it, be gentle, confess a time that you were called on and didn't know the answer, and mail everyone chocolate afterwards.

However, all the chocolate in the world won't help if your presentation is bad. So remember to apply the basics: thoroughly research your topic and organize your material, punch up your key points with emotionally potent examples, and practice, practice, practice. Enunciate and speak directly into the mic (confirmation that your audience can hear you is a good idea). If you're using a webcam, your silent message is back in play, and now includes everything in the background, so make sure the camera is capturing your face and torso—not just the top of your hair and ceiling. Unless you have hair like Vanilla Ice did in the 90s, in which case zoom in on that glorious mane.

Look at the camera as much as you can to simulate eye contact. Looking at the lens rather than your screen will make your delivery feel more intimate, though the audience may not be able to articulate why.

Last, minimize background noise and distractions. With a four-year-old on the loose, my home office isn't the most silent of studios. But Noah's noisy playtimes are a blessing and burden I gladly accept, and the rest of the family does an excellent job keeping him quiet(ish) anytime I'm leading an important call.

In fact, the last time someone crashed a remote meeting on my end the culprit wasn't kids, but livestock. An unseasonably warm February afternoon, I had my office windows open, and when my neighbor delivered some hay (did I mention that I live in the sticks?), his cows thanked him with moos of joy. I thought they were too far away for my mic to pick up. But their bellows of lunchtime joy echoed throughout the valley, all the way to the attendees' speakers. "Matt, are those *cows* in the background?" "Yeah, sorry about that. They were hungry."

Key Takeaways

➲ PowerPoint is a **visual** aid—less text, more pictures

➲ Engaging a remote audience is **doubly** important

➲ If you practice with a pretend mic, **do it in secret**

➲ Beware of **interrupting cows**

Part IV

Always
Improving

Chapter Thirteen

LESS READING, MORE SPEAKING

Experienced painters begin somewhere inconspicuous, like in a closet. Once they've confirmed the color works, then they'll turn to the living room. Similarly, top college football programs will schedule low-ranked opponents early in the season to work out the kinks before the big games later in the year. And smart swimming students practice in the shallow end with arm floaties until they get the hang of it. The principle: hone your skills where the stakes are low, *then* tackle the more important work.

I'd like to give you the chance to develop as a speaker in a similar fashion: slowly, beginning with simple, easy opportunities, where it doesn't matter if you mess up. You can adopt the plan that follows wholesale, or customize it. The only thing that isn't optional is whether you present.

The time to commit to and plan your next (or first) talk is now. Not after you finish the book, not when you've finished some class, not when the stars perfectly align—now.

No more delays. No more excuses. Swimmers must swim and speakers must speak. Commit to and schedule your next presentation before you move on to the next chapter, just so you're reassured that your effort here hasn't been wasted. Don't worry—it doesn't have to be especially fancy, as you'll soon see.

We'll begin with confidence-building speaking opportunities that are fully doable today, regardless of your experience. These "quick wins" may seem insignificant, but depending on how much public speaking you've done, they could prove the difference between building the momentum to finally achieve your potential or continuing to run from it.

Then we'll branch into opportunities that are slightly more formal, with slightly larger crowds, on slightly more complex topics, and with slightly higher stakes. You'll find the step into "stretch assignments" fun and exciting, for by the time you get there, you'll be ready for the challenge. You may even be ready right now.

Then with multiple live presentations under your belt, you'll be ready for "show time"—the reason you're doing all this work. This is only bound by your imagination. So aim high—no reason to settle for office briefs if theatre is in your heart.

QUICK WINS

Low-risk and to a small audience, quick wins are what their title implies: fast and easy ways to build your public speaking experience and confidence.

This is super simple stuff, and if you're a novice, this is a wonderful place to begin your public speaking journey. No more procrastination. No more excuses. Decide to dominate, and let's go.

1. Checkout Speech

If you're in need of networking advice, Susan RoAne's *How to Work a Room* is an excellent resource, chock-full of practical tips on how to navigate most any social engagement.[7]

For example, anytime you find yourself among strangers, seek out and introduce yourself to people who are alone, and especially people who are alone and look uncomfortable. Why? They're probably lonely, and will welcome your company.

RoAne recommends that before you try using her tips at a presidential dinner, you should practice on a captive

---

[7] This is the book with the name-remembering association trick from chapter six.

audience likely to welcome friendly conversation—such as a grocery store clerk.

Rather than making small talk, your assignment here is to covertly deliver a prepared (though brief) presentation. That's right—I'm asking you to develop, rehearse and deliver a talk to the Walmart cashier (or Whole Foods for my hipster friends).

Make your mini-talk about something of mutual interest, such as the sale on cucumbers, or maybe the weather. Or swap recipes. "Have you tried this chili mix? My mother always added cumin and…" is a great way to start. Then roll into your prepared sub-points on achieving the perfect combination of spice and cheese. Or convince them to form a union and overthrow their corporate overlords (my grandfather was a union organizer). Make it fun!

If you feel a little weird doing this, good—that means you're normal. But only you will know. The cashier will just think you're friendly.

The more depth and complexity you build in, the better. But for now, just get it out. The point is to get some experience following a mental outline, and to build a little assertiveness. Public speaking nervousness is often caused by general shyness, and not only will this first exercise build your social comfort, it will brighten some lucky cashier's day.

2. Your Story

Develop, revise, rehearse and find opportunities to share your unique story. You're the author of this story, so make it a pleasure to both hear and tell.

For example, two important events happened to me soon after getting out of the Air Force: I got laid off from a job (which gave me motivation to turn a side gig into a fulltime business… the sweatiness of which gave me the motivation to try college), and I started dating my sister's best friend (whom I wed three years later). Both events were important, and while I put a positive spin on getting downsized, people always seem to prefer the love story. And just as importantly, I always prefer to tell it. Make your story a happy one, too.

Once it's ready, rehearse (continuing to revise), and put yourself in settings where people will be invited to introduce themselves. Have a rough outline in your head, preferably ordered chronologically, and unpack it as you go. This exercise is not only great public speaking practice, it may help you better understand where you've been, where you are, and where you're going.

Here's mine: "I grew up on a horse farm in East Tennessee, did a few years in the Air Force, moved back home and started a parking lot maintenance business, gave college a shot in my mid-20s, and came out ten years later with a Ph.D. in philosophy, specializing in social & political philosophy and applied ethics. Married to my sister's best friend and with three kids, my work as a management analyst currently pays the mortgage, but my real passions are writing and speaking. I'm happiest outdoors, fulfilled a lifelong dream to competitively box and kickbox before I turned 40, and just finished building my family's 'forever home' on that same horse farm where I grew up. Find me online at MattDeaton.com."

Simple, to the point, and overall happy. Type up your own, rehearse it until it feels smooth and natural, and be ready to deliver it the next time someone offers the invitation, "So tell us a bit about yourself…"

STRETCH ASSIGNMENTS

With a couple of quick wins under your belt, now's the time to increase your audience size and up the stakes. Just a little.

3. Library Volunteer

As the title implies, this assignment involves volunteering at your local library. If yours holds weekly story times for kids, sign up to help with the next one. If it doesn't, volunteer to organize and host one next Saturday at noon. (That's right—I said *next Saturday at noon.* No excuses!)

Preparing is easy. You're just going to read a children's book aloud. But be sure to practice holding the book at an angle that will allow you to see the words while the kids can still see the pictures—this is one of the few times it's actually preferable to read from a script.

Once you're comfortable with the basic storyline and have read it aloud a couple of times, try bringing the characters to life. Put some bass into the Big Bad Wolf's huffs and puffs. Give the troll a smoker's cough, and the Billy Goats Gruff voices that match their sizes.

I'm assigning this because I used to read children's stories to third and fourth graders as part of a Philosophy for Kids program at an underprivileged elementary school, and the experience did wonders for my growth as a speaker. Although kids are an appreciative audience, they're also honest, and their attention spans short.

As I learned, presenting to kids makes you work on eye contact, voice inflection, movement, and general audience engagement. But the beauty is that if you're not a hit, who cares—they're just a bunch of kids! You get the growth benefits regardless.

So give it a try. And feel free to modify the assignment to suit your circumstances. Do something similar at a Boys & Girls Club, the kid care at your gym, your church, etc. But if you're to stay true to the method, it needs to happen within the next week. (If that feels scary, stop it— they're just kids!)

4. Big Idea

Think of a way to improve something that will require others' support. It could be at work, at church, knitting class, some club thing you do—your choice.

Once you've identified your big idea, develop, revise and practice a presentation on it (doesn't have to be long), and schedule a time to pitch it. In fact, schedule a time to pitch it *first*, then develop the presentation. Public commitment to do it and a date on the calendar will ensure you actually get it done.

This presentation should be brief and will have a very basic structure: 1) Here's the issue background, 2) here's the specific problem I'd like to address, 3) here's my suggested solution, 4) here's why this solution is better than others, and by the way, 5) here's how I need you to help.

Since this is only a stretch assignment, you can make your presentation as formal or as informal as you like. Just remember that the point is twofold: to communicate a valuable solution and grow as a speaker. No pressure to cure cancer. Just a speaking stretch assignment.

5. Family Prayer

I once taught at a Christian university where students expected professors to begin class with a prayer. With zero experience doing this at the time (and worried that my students' religious understandings might not perfectly match my own), this was intimidating. But I obliged (usually—sometimes I'd punt to the class), and the more I did it, the easier it got.

Before COVID hit, I as studying Isshinryu Karate with all three of my kids, and at the beginning of each class the sensei would ask someone to lead a group prayer. While I was caught off guard the first time Mr. Ogle tapped me to pray, soon it became no big deal, and I was always honored. We're still training, by the way. Except now, for the time being, it's in the garage rather than the dojo.

Where am I going with this? ("Where am I going with this?" is a transition pastor Joel Osteen uses often. He's as smooth a presenter as they come, and inspirational—

check him out.) Leading prayer has been such an awkward challenge for me, a guy who's otherwise comfortable in front of a crowd, that I'd like you to use it as a stretch assignment. Who knows, maybe you'll grow spiritually, too.

If you and your family happen to be religious, prepare (and rehearse) a brief, simple, but sincere prayer for your next gathering, and recite it before the meal. If you and your family happen to not be religious, same assignment—just keep your eyes open and address your loved ones directly.

If you're having trouble finding inspiration, share how blessed you feel to have one another, how grateful you are for the food, and how eager you are to eat it. (You are eager to eat it, aren't you?)

If the idea feels weird, it felt weird for me, too. While I've prayed with more or less regularity since I was a kid, it's always been a silent, private thing, which has made doing it aloud in public a rewarding challenge.

I want the same benefits for you. And don't worry that your personal theology might differ from the theology of the people you're leading. It probably does. But as long as you're not praying to trees (hipsters—I'm looking at you), no one's likely to notice, let alone care.

SHOW TIME!

You've done enough studying and practicing. It's show time.

6. Open Mic

Ah, open mic night at the local comedy club. Here we go—it's time for a real audience, a real microphone, and some real expectations. But to lessen that pressure, I'm giving you permission to do something typically considered an unforgivable comedic sin. Rather than spending the *enormous* amount of time it takes to author, refine, and perfect a quality original routine, just copy some of your favorite comedians' jokes.

Usually this would constitute plagiarism. The only way you're able to get away with it here is that you're going to announce up front that the jokes you're telling aren't your own, and give credit to the original author or performer. Just explain that you're not there to become the next Jerry Seinfeld, but because "Professor Matt" (my old comedy stage name) told you doing open mics was a great way to grow as a public speaker.

Normal public speaking is already fun, but there's nothing like making a room full of people burst into physical joy with your words (even if they're words borrowed from someone else). That instant and emphatic group approval is satisfying on an instinctual level.

All that said, you are welcome to tell your own jokes. And if you happen to catch the comedy bug, check out Greg Dean's *Step by Step to Stand-Up Comedy* or Judy Carter's *Stand-Up Comedy: The Book*. Both are excellent places for aspiring comedians to begin

Steve Martin's MasterClass is also an excellent resource, and includes a coaching session where he works with four young comics, reads some of their material aloud, and helps them revise it. One of Martin's tips is consistent with what we've covered here—less is more, cut the clutter, streamline. He's brutally honest about what material is distracting filler and what actually adds funny, and encourages the comics to ruthlessly cut the fluff.

Again, you're free to borrow existing jokes and use this exercise as a way to expand your comfort zone, not launch a comedy career. But it could happen... One of the dudes I used to do open mics with in Knoxville is hitting the big time— Trae Crowder aka "The Liberal Redneck." Back in the day Trae was "The Corporate Redneck," but he had to get enough experience to uncover his authentic stage self. He's doing something right, for recently the great Morgan Freeman said in an interview that Trae made him laugh. If the idea of an aggressively left-leaning hillbilly sounds like your idea of funny, Trae might make you laugh, too. Just beware of the language.

7. Why You Picked Up the Book

You picked up this book with some idea of when, where and how you'd like to speak publicly. A sneaky voice has been trying to convince you that my calls to act don't apply to you—that I'm OK with you skipping all these assignments, that you need to read two or three or even four more public speaking books before you'll be ready to speak.

Whatever. By the time you've read this far and completed the growth assignments above (maybe just one of them), you'll be more than ready to tackle your original goal.

I can say with confidence that you'll be ready enough because waiting until you feel *fully* ready is deadly. It's deadly because our time on this planet is limited, and if we wait for conditions to be perfect, we'll wait until we're dead.

Even if your performance is on the bleh side (if you apply what you're learning, it won't be), there will be more opportunities to shine, and you will improve as you go. We're all works in progress. So don't procrastinate. All the time you've spent studying and pondering is wasted if you never do the thing you were aiming for all along.

You're even welcome (and encouraged) to jump straight to this step if you like. I'm the last person who wants to stall your growth with baby steps if you don't need them. If you're willing to put yourself out there sooner rather than later, let's do it! Everything you need is either within you or on these pages—most of it, within you.

8. Go Bigger!

I'm sure your original speaking goal was impressive when you made it. But with all you're learning and doing, don't you think you're setting the bar kinda low? I do. Now dream bigger.

And don't just dream, for dreams—when they remain dreams—*are for suckers.* Dream, plan, act, *realize.* Speaking for cool audiences on cool occasions is a thrill and source of esteem that will open doors and enrich your life in ways you cannot imagine.

If I can do it, you can do it. Begin with that checkout speech, lead a family prayer, conquer your original goal (or skip right to it). Then with all you're learning and applying, and with all that momentum, I dare you to see how far you can take this. Your only limits are self-imposed. Let that bad wolf nonsense go, and embrace the uncertain awesomeness that awaits.

Bonus Assignment

9. YouTuber

Before the assignment title runs you off, know that there's a way to make any YouTube video private (so no one can see it unless they have the password) or unlisted (meaning anyone can watch it with the direct URL, but it won't show up in searches). While it is true that anything you upload to the web (even in private or unlisted mode) might someday be unearthed, this is a simple growth opportunity, you're going to do great, and people are too busy watching clips of cats to pay attention to your public speaking practice vid.

The assignment: make a 2-5-minute tutorial on anything you like. Research, develop your message and rehearse as you would for a live, in-person talk. But then record it instead. Pick something you already enjoy and understand, or something you'd really like to learn about.

Follow the message development steps from the Know Thy Material chapter, then write your outline on a Post-It note and affix it beneath your smartphone's self-facing lens (or on your selfie stick handle/tripod if you have one—if not, no worries). By the third or fourth take, you probably won't need notes. But having the outline within view is reassuring, and nice when needed.

The beauty of this assignment is twofold. People could eventually see it, so there's pressure to do a good job. But it's on something you already know and like (or at least something you're excited to be learning about), plus you get to decide which take gets uploaded. If things don't come out perfectly the first (or fifteenth) time, hit stop and begin again. For every video that made it onto YouTube.com/MattDeatonPhD, there were two, three, sometimes a dozen that I started, didn't like, deleted and rerecorded. Recording a philosophical ethics video in Central Park, I was photo-bombed by rats. Huge, fearless NYC rats terrorizing the tourists. The rats version did not make it to YouTube. Neither did any of the versions where I mispronounced something or tripped and cursed. You exercise similar control over what makes it online and what doesn't, so chill and have fun with this.

If you do it and would like some feedback, share the URL using the contact form at MattDeaton.com. I'll be kind, but honest, so only ask for feedback if you're cool with constructive coaching. You'll probably be awesome, but just in case… Either way, there's certainly no pressure to be perfect. Goodness knows my videos aren't perfect. So pick a cool topic, and have fun.

Maybe this will ignite your worldwide YouTuber celebrity! Regardless, it will accelerate your speaking growth, and give your stage chutzpah a nice boost. But it's optional. In fact, everything in this book is optional, including the assignments in this chapter. If you don't have time for all this, pick two that feel right and do your best. Just remember: swimmers must swim.

Key Takeaways

⮑ **Checkout Speech**: Grow as a speaker as you brighten your cashier's day

⮑ **Your Story**: Author and share a happy autobiography

⮑ **Library Volunteer**: Read books to kids—*The Giving Tree* is a good one

⮑ **Big Idea**: Share your idea to improve something

⮑ **Family Prayer**: Be ready for Thanksgiving with an earnest prayer

⮑ **Open Mic**: No pressure to be hilarious or even original—just practicing

⮑ **Why You Picked Up the Book**: Whatever presentation you had in mind when you started reading, go do it!

⮑ **Go Bigger**: And don't just dream—act

⮑ **YouTuber Bonus**: A video on a cool topic of your choice, with optional feedback from Professor Matt

Chapter Fourteen

THE COMMITMENT
TO GET BETTER

Successful entrepreneurs study past sales, anticipate market changes, and adjust their products accordingly. Successful politicians study policy platforms that have won elections (and those that haven't), poll current preferences, and adjust their campaigns to match. Successful sports coaches watch game film, anticipate upcoming opponents' strategies, and adjust their lineup and plays to give them the best chance to win. The lesson: self-assess and proactively improve.

For every talk you give, reflect on what went well, what didn't, and how you can build on your strengths and address your weaknesses. This is the path to realizing your best public speaking self.

Two Case Studies

Here are a couple of self-analyses of my own presentations. For the first, I was asked to brief my boss's boss on the vision and values portion of our office's strategic plan. Main upshot? I found the experience more nerve-wracking than expected, which taught me some important lessons about preparing exactly as I'll deliver. But it also reaffirmed my ability to work through bouts of nervousness when they strike.

Boss's Boss Brief

Preparation: Drafted presentation slides and talking points on Wednesday. Rehearsed solo six times on Thursday and three times on Friday.

Monday Morning Dress Rehearsal: Sat around a large conference table with half a dozen colleagues—felt fine going in, but heart sped up as my turn to speak approached. By the time I began speaking it was racing, so much so that my voice quivered. Not sure why!

Monday Afternoon Real Thing: Sat around a small conference table with same colleagues—not nearly as nervous as during dry run, but failed to elaborate on key points as planned. Interruptions from boss's boss threw off delivery.

Analysis:

Observation A: The dress rehearsal helped. Taking the time to practice around a similar table with my presentation partners made the real thing easier, especially since I have lots of experience presenting solo while standing, but very little experience presenting as part of a group sitting down.

Lessons:

1. Do a dress rehearsal every time—better to have first-time foul-ups during practice than the real thing.

Observation B: Presenting sitting down felt very awkward—especially around a small table in a small room. And while I practiced several times beforehand, almost every time I did it standing up.

Lessons:

1. Practice exactly as you will speak, whether that's seated, standing, using a lectern, not using a lectern, with a mic, without a mic, etc.
2. Volunteer for more seated speaking opportunities to shore up that area of my speaking game.

Observation C: I got much more nervous than expected. Maybe because I was new to the office? Maybe because I didn't fully appreciate the material's background? Maybe because I was infected by others' nervousness?

Lessons:

1. Despite your newness and the hierarchy, remember that you're pretty awesome—never let the perceived opinion of others impact your self-esteem.
2. Know Thy Material—be sure to fully understand the material you're responsible for presenting, including background context.
3. Be the Fonz—strive to serve as a role model of cool and calm rather than letting the nervousness of others drag you down.

As you can see, some things went well, some didn't. By reflecting on both, I was able to illuminate lessons learned, which enabled me to adjust preparation for future presentations, and become an even better speaker.

I gave that presentation on a Monday afternoon. Here's an analysis of a welcome speech I gave the following Saturday at American University as host of the inaugural Washington DC Area High School Ethics Bowl. Co-organizing the DC Ethics

Bowl was a side project I had worked on for several months, and one that was in jeopardy of falling apart at several stages (Will we have enough teams? Will we have enough judges? Will we have a place to hold it?). But by the time the bowl arrived, it was clear it would be a success. It was just a matter of execution.

DC Ethics Bowl

Preparation: Spent most of my free time the week prior confirming volunteer participation, selecting cases, printing materials, and otherwise handling logistics. I didn't sketch an official outline until late Friday, which I briefly rehearsed while getting ready the next morning, and again on my way to the event. Spent time self-coaching, deciding that not only would my opening speech go well, but so would the entire event. I visualized how much fun the participants would have, and how satisfied I'd feel once it was over.

Show Time: The joy of seeing the bowl come together and my focus on greeting guests prevented my nerves from acting up beforehand. The crowd was very positive and enthusiastic—so much so that my opening line, "Welcome to the inaugural Washington DC Area High School Ethics Bowl" was met with cheers and applause! That unexpected response created a wave of enthusiasm that carried me through my main points. Though my transitions could have been smoother, and I forgot the names of a couple of people I intended to thank, it was overall a very successful presentation.

Analysis:

Observation A: I was very comfortable presenting solo, standing, and being able to walk around. Felt like I was back in the college classroom.

Lessons:

1. Building on my strengths, I should present under these conditions more often.

Observation B: The audience's enthusiasm fueled my confidence.

Lessons:

1. Always present on happy topics to happy people!
2. When the above isn't possible, expect the audience to be happy, and anytime they're obviously not (tapping their foot and scowling), *imagine* that they're happy—should have a similar effect (fuel my confidence).

Observation C: Forgot a few key names. Whoops!

Lessons:

1. Use notes for unfamiliar key info—much better to read a coach's name from a slip of paper than have to ask the audience.

As you can see, I had room for improvement (always do). Couldn't believe I forgot those names... But overall it was a huge success, and I learned some valuable lessons in the process—key details on a slip of paper in my pocket (or in the PowerPoint notes), just in case.

It takes extra time and effort to reflect on your performances and improve. But it works. Six months after that boss's boss speech, I was back in the same room, this time presenting to my boss's *boss's* boss and a team of other bosses— what should have been a much more intimidating audience. But in part thanks to lessons I learned from the first time around, I'm proud to say I felt great going in, and absolutely *nailed* that presentation. I had only rehearsed once, but it was sitting down, and this time I really understood the topic. Lesson: practice exactly as you'll perform and know thy material. Like a boss.

If my experience isn't enough, look to top athletes for confirmation that performance analysis is worth the trouble. Win or lose, most spend the entire first working day after a game watching film. They study what they did poorly, but also what they did well. Then they scout their next opponent, come up with a customized plan to correct their weaknesses and build on their strengths, and get to work. If you're serious about achieving your potential, do the same.

Key Takeaways

➲ Learn from and improve after **every** presentation

➲ Practice **exactly** as you'll perform

➲ Have notes on **standby** for key details

➲ Mitigate your weaknesses and **build** on your strengths

➲ Be the **Fonz**

Chapter Fifteen

MINDSET REVISITED

In the conquering nervousness chapter we covered the importance of releasing the negative, amplifying the positive, Focusing where it Matters and Acting where it Counts (FM-AC). You learned how to improve your psyche by adjusting your posture, the power of affirmations, and how to fake it 'til you make it. You also learned a slightly unconventional assertiveness drill, which you've since practiced on the mailman.

But there's more to developing a winning public speaking mindset than positive self-talk and biting off bad guys' nipples. For example, there's transcending the crippling curse of perfectionism.

IT AIN'T A GRAND PIANO

"It ain't a grand piano." That's the phrase Rita Emmett, author of *The Procrastinator's Handbook: Mastering the Art of Doing It Now*, tells us carpenters use to reset anytime they catch themselves fretting over minor flaws.

It's appropriate to obsess over selecting the right wood, measuring, re-measuring, cutting, re-cutting, sanding, re-sanding—ensuring everything is *just right*—when building a grand piano, for grand pianos are works of art. However, most carpentry projects are not grand pianos.

Most of our presentations aren't grand pianos. They're of course not dingy bookshelves, either. But it's foolish (not to mention frustrating) to demand perfection when the project doesn't warrant it. And even when the project does warrant it, perfection is only an ideal to pursue, not an achievable end.

Emmett's advice: aim for *excellence* rather than perfection in everything you do, which in our case includes organizing our material, tailoring our silent message, rehearsing, delivering. We'll not only overcome perfectionist-driven procrastination by choosing excellence instead. We'll have a better time doing it.

Still decide to dominate, still commit to realizing your best public speaking self. Just know that excellence is the standard, not perfection.

UPROOT SUBCONSCIOUS SABOTAGE

Sometimes the biggest mental obstacle isn't fear of failure, but fear of success. While we might consciously want to succeed, our subconscious might worry about side effects like increased responsibility or raised expectations. And when the conscious mind wants something the subconscious mind resists, self-sabotage is a predictable result.

For example, I used to open my comedy set with the following joke:

> I go by "Professor Matt" on stage because I really am a professor. And I hate it when people find that out and get all paranoid about their grammar. Look—*I'm* the professor—the pressure's on *me* to be grammatically perfect. Everyone else: *you're free to appear just as ignorant as you actually are.*

This joke made *me* smile, but it often offended my audience. And since it's hard to laugh when you're offended, this wasn't a smart joke to include at all, let alone open with. So why in the world did I continue to use it until a mentor convinced me to stop?

Although I was never in danger of being whisked away to Hollywood, I remember thinking how much travel rising comedians have to endure while building their fan base, and how incompatible that seemed with a rich family life. The comics who came through town for weekend shows were usually exhausted, having just driven several hundred miles from their last gig, and about to drive several hundred more to their next.

As a local club host, while I didn't get paid much, my commute was 30 minutes. Even though I enjoyed the glamour of the spotlight and the thrill of making an audience laugh, I knew it would never be more than a hobby—any career that required long stretches away from my young and growing family wasn't a career for me. So maybe I stuck with that insulting opener for so long because it was my subconscious mind's way of ensuring I was never tempted to go on tour.

If you find the idea of public speaking unsettling, maybe the root cause isn't the speaking itself, but some potential consequence—like a new job that might require an unwanted move, or new responsibilities you're not sure you can handle. Maybe your best friend is a terrible speaker, and you're subconsciously worried that if you become a speaking star their jealousy will destroy your relationship. Or maybe your mother wants you to become a pastor, you want to remain an accountant, and your subconscious fears that if you could speak, you'd have one less excuse to avoid seminary.

Whatever tricks your mind might be playing, reflect to attain what Freud called "insight." Is there something about becoming a successful speaker that scares or intimidates you? Not failing, but *succeeding?*

Give that some thought, and reassure yourself by debunking dubious pitfalls. Nailing a presentation might very well open new doors. But job offers can be refused, your best friend is more likely to be proud of you than jealous, and Mom's going to pressure you to join the clergy regardless.

CHALLENGES = OPPORTUNITIES TO GROW

Students sometimes view college as a bureaucratic obstacle between them and a better job. "I'm pre-med. How's American Literature supposed to help me become an orthopedic surgeon?"

I'll admit that I once viewed my non-major classes this way. But as I worked my way through them, I began to see them not as hoops through which I had to jump, but as opportunities to learn. And with the help of many excellent professors, I came to see them not only as opportunities to learn, but to grow.

American Literature wasn't an employment scam for English professors. Well, it was... But it was also a chance to read some of the most powerful and wisdom-filled stories ever written. Western Civilization wasn't a cluster of random facts and dates. Well, it was... But it was also a chance to understand and better participate in the political and social world around me. And Intro to Philosophy wasn't pointless musings about the unanswerable. It was a fortuitous chance to discover a passion for reason-guided thought that would lead to the switching of majors, and a completely different life trajectory. (If you've enjoyed this book, thank Socrates, for I doubt orthopedic surgeon Matt would have found time to speak, let alone write a speaking book.)

To the extent that I looked at my classes as opportunities rather than burdens, I got more out of them. And when I became a teacher myself, I tried to encourage my students— many of whom were taking my own class as a non-major distribution requirement—to do the same. Those who have always seem happier and to grow more.

Viewing an otherwise stressful speaking engagement in this way is helpful in terms of whether you'll enjoy it, how well you'll do, and the person you'll be on the other side. If you prepare and expect to do well, you likely will. But whatever the case, if you're going to do it regardless, embrace it. What seems outside your comfort zone today could be fully within it next week. It's all a matter of whether you're willing to grow.

SETBACKS = OPPORTUNITIES TO LEARN

About three years after my first public speaking class, where I had grinned my way through a Timothy McVeigh speech, I was in front of a classroom again—this time as a graduate teaching assistant charged with leading a weekly discussion section for an Intro to Philosophy class.

Being on the teaching side was an honor, but also intimidating. So I typed up paragraphs-long lectures, projected them onto the whiteboard, and stood at the back of the room (where no one could see me) and read them aloud. Verbatim. With no visuals or adlibbing. Former students, my deepest apologies. I believe that's what they call "Death by PowerPoint."

Three years later I was making my comedy debut at my very first open mic, and my set's opening joke was greeted with blank stares and crickets. I'd read books on comedy, spent hours developing what I thought was an awesome set, and had put what I considered my best material first as the professionals advised. But somehow the crowd just did not get my gun safety joke.

> The first rule of firearms safety is to never point your weapon at anything you wouldn't want to destroy. And that's really the *only* firearms safety rule you need... unless you're Godzilla!

Godzilla, of course, wants to destroy *everything*, so this rule wouldn't give him any useful safety guidance, right? Because he's a raging monster, and *enjoys* destruction, and... oh, forget it.

Those were low points on my speaking journey. But each was a transformative learning opportunity. By the end of that first public speaking class I'd learned the importance of being myself (no more grinning like an idiot when the material didn't call for it). By the end of that philosophy class I'd realized that my job wasn't to prevent students from discovering what I didn't know, but to clearly convey what I did (idea transfer, baby). And as I worked through my set that first evening on the comedy stage, I learned the value of perseverance. While the Godzilla joke bombed, the rest of my set did not, and by the time my six minutes were up, I'd earned cheers from the crowd and hearty congrats from my fellow amateur comedians.

The lessons don't always come easy. But with every survived mistake, mustering the courage to climb onto bigger stages with bigger stakes gets easier.

You're bound to have your own Godzilla moments. When they happen, be glad. Bearing the disapproving glares of hipsters in an art studio sucked. (Ya'll really liked the interpretive dancer better than me? The poem guy, too?) But setbacks are part of the process, and if met with the right attitude, will make you a better speaker. Maybe even a better person.

FOCUS ON THE FIX

Top business schools teach MBA students on day one that "No business plan survives first contact with the customer." And it was Iron Mike Tyson who said, "Everybody has a plan until they get punched in the mouth."

Public speaking isn't as unpredictable as business or as violent as boxing. Only occasionally will things go wrong, and almost never will someone punch you in the mouth. Especially if you avoid those face tattoos.

However, if you speak often and long enough, you'll eventually run into unexpected trouble. After these experiences are over, I of course recommend using them as learning opportunities. But as they're happening, and while you can still do something about them, be solution-oriented.

A friend who works at the Department of Defense was briefing a manager on encryption technology. The topic was complex, and the manager just wasn't getting it. But rather than asking my friend for clarification or repeating back to her what she thought was being said, the manager responded by burying her face in her hands and saying, "I'll come back to this next week—I'm just too busy right now."

My friend was at a complete loss. She'd studied. She'd prepared. She'd practiced. But her audience was frustrated and unreceptive, apparently unwilling to meet her halfway. She reluctantly agreed to reschedule the presentation and try again. But could she have done anything better? How about this:

> Ma'am, if it turns out we really do need to reschedule, I'm happy to come back. But since we're here and have the time, let's give this one more shot. I'll make it more of a conversation than a lecture. And maybe if I can better understand what *is* clear, I can better understand what isn't, and we can work together to fill in the gaps. Cool?

Maybe the manager would have insisted on rescheduling. But the point is that my friend had more attractive options. Of course, I've not always handled setbacks so well myself.

I remember presenting a draft paper to UT's Philosophy Department late one Friday afternoon. The football team was scheduled to play the Air Force Academy the next day, and right in the middle of my presentation a squadron of low-flying jets buzzed campus—apparently a pre-game tactic used by Air Force brass to intimidate opposing teams.

Those planes weren't just loud. *They shook the building.* And though I tried to talk on through, there was no way I could have held a flight crew's attention, let alone an audience of philosophy professors and grad students. It would have been much better had I paused, acknowledged the distraction, and continued once the pilots had had their fun.

Three years later, I did a little better when I walked onto the comedy club stage and found a dead mic. There I was, the center of attention for dozens of paying customers who'd just been whipped into a frenzy by the video the club played at the beginning of each show, and my one essential piece of technology was failing.

With the stage lights amplifying my every expression, I'm sure they could see my eyes widen and my face redden as my enthusiasm turned to fear. But rather than stalling or running away, I put the mic back into its stand, moved it to the side, took a deep breath, and began my opening monologue per usual—only louder so folks in the back could hear.

Adding a quip about the cheap owners and the electric bill would have been even better. But I was able to work through the equipment failure because I immediately focused on solutions. Troy the sound man/engineer/bouncer rushed to the stage and had the mic working in no time, and when he gave the thumbs up I retrieved it from the stand and kept going.

The point of the noisy jets fail and dead mic win stories isn't to make you think problems are inevitable. They're not. I've spoken on hundreds of occasions, and only recall a handful of negative experiences. Most of the time mics work as they should and jets maintain an appropriate altitude.

But on the rare occasion hiccups do occur, just shift into solution mode. If the power goes out, you can get flustered and quit. Or you can use your cellphone as a flashlight and continue until maintenance comes to the rescue. Invite the audience to turn theirs on, too—I guarantee they'd pay attention and remember you. If the building catches fire, you can scream and run in a circle like SpongeBob. Or you can coordinate an orderly evacuation and continue your talk in the parking lot.

Expect things to go exceedingly well, not only because both positive and negative prophecies tend to self-fulfill, but because from my experience, genuine setbacks are rare. So long as you've prepared and practiced, and especially if you've tested your equipment, you'll be fine. And on the rare occasion that things do go wrong, take a deep breath, focus on the fix, and press on through.

Key Takeaways

- ⊃ Aim for **excellence**

- ⊃ Ensure dubious **subconscious** worries aren't undermining your goals

- ⊃ Use challenges to **grow** and setbacks to **learn**

- ⊃ Focus on the **fix**

Chapter Sixteen

PAID TO SPEAK?

If you continue to invest the time to improve your craft, audiences will notice. One day someone may surprise you with a question about your availability and speaking fees.

That you could speak (semi-)professionally might sound crazy. But polished, authentic, topic-flexible speakers are rare, so don't rule it out. It may not cover the mortgage at first. But whether it's for $50 or $5,000, getting paid to do something once terrifying is super fun.

HAREN'S SECRET: DELIVER QUALITY WORK

Speaking pro bono to gain the experience and exposure is a fair trade when you're starting out. And if you're willing to speak for free forever, you'll certainly find venues that will let you.

But your time and skills are valuable, and at some point you should be able to negotiate monetary compensation.

Exactly when will turn largely on how much you'll need to make it worth your while versus how badly potential clients want you in particular. But if you want to increase the value you offer, Fredrik Haren says that the most important thing you can do is simply deliver great presentations.

He makes this a staple of his book *Spread Your Message. See the World. How to Become a Global Keynote Speaker* and ensures his readers remember it by closing every chapter with the reminder: "The key to building a successful speaking career is a really great speech, which will lead to people booking you again. It's that simple."

From my experience, he's right. Most of my gigs are either repeat customers or people who attended one of my talks. I owe my local chamber of commerce a *huge* thank you for inviting me to speak at their events. "An audience full of potential clients? Why yes, I'd be happy to keynote your business appreciation breakfast." Brandy and Karen, I am in forever your debt.

But even when the leads are less obvious, your first or next paying customer could be in the audience of any presentation you give. So if you're enticed by the business possibilities, treat every presentation (in part) as a job interview, and remember

216

Haren's advice that nothing grows a speaking business like a quality presentation.

MONEY TALKS

Alan Weiss's *Money Talks* is packed with practical advice for the aspiring professional, and definitely worth your while if you'd like to make money at this. But two tips that stood out for me were 1) make sure your talk satisfies whoever's paying the bill, and 2) make sure the focus is your audience, not you.

On the first, get in touch with the CEO or the owner or whoever's ultimately paying your fee. This may not be the person who initially contacts you (likely an administrative employee or event planner). But if you'd like the true boss's recommendation (and repeat business), don't simply please the middleperson.

Research the company, make some calls, figure out who's in charge and do whatever it takes to match (or best) their vision. However, do this tactfully. Chances are good that your point of contact will welcome your interest in pleasing their boss. Let them help you, respect their chain of command, and don't be too eager to go over their head.

On Weiss's second point, whatever the topic, deliver it in a way that makes it not only relevant to your audience, but as directly about them as possible. Why? People are generally self-absorbed—the hero of their own personal story. If your talk doesn't reference, apply to or help them, they're unlikely to care.

This is essentially the same message that marketing consultant Donald Miller offers in *Building a StoryBrand: Clarify Your Message So Customers Will Listen*. Miller wasn't talking about public speaking when he cautioned companies to ensure that their brand positions the customer as the hero. But the logic holds.

Miller illustrates his advice with an analysis of Apple. When Apple ran a multi-page ad in the New York Times in 1983 to tout the specs of its new "Lisa" desktop, sales were sluggish. Lisa was a fine machine, but the average consumer couldn't understand the technical jargon in the ad, let alone see how it would assist their personal hero's journey.

Then Steve Jobs left the company to run Pixar Studios (producer of some of my kids' favorite movies, including the Monsters Inc. franchise), where he learned about crafting a good story, and apparently a thing or two about product positioning. When he returned, Apple's marketing shifted from highlighting the equipment to highlighting the user.

Apple continued to turn out quality products with impressive specs. "Notice, though, the story of Apple isn't about Apple; it's about you. You're the hero in the story, and they play the role more like Q in the James Bond movies. They are the guy you go to see when you need a tool to help you win the day" (19).

As a speaker, your ego will try to rationalize why thinly veiled bragging is actually a crowd pleaser. For example, I was flattered to be invited to give a goal accomplishment talk to 8th graders at the local middle school. *"Moi?* Teach the youth goal accomplishment and personal success? It would be my utmost pleasure."

I reasoned that the better the students appreciated the fact that I was from their town and an alumnus of their school, the more receptive they'd be to my golden advice. So I started my presentation with school pictures. "Here's me in 1st grade. Here's me as a Cub Scout in the 3rd grade. And here's me at your age, unfortunately with a mullet. I hope none of you have mullets…"

This was enough to make the "I'm one of you" connection I was after. However, my ego got the best of me, and the first *twenty-three* slides were pictures of me: me on the school basketball team, me on a dirt bike, teenage me crouched beside my green '75 Coupe Deville (dressed like a thug), me with my graduating class. I even included college graduation pictures, wedding pictures, screen shots of my YouTube videos, me in DC, me in the Air Force, me coaching baseball, me doing stand-up comedy, me with a deer I hit on my way to teach at a rural community college (I guess I thought the dead deer would impress the hunters).

This is embarrassing to admit. And the slides are tough to look at today. But like you, on stage and off, I'm a work in progress. Today I double-check my presentations to ensure that they're about and for the audience, and that self-references serve a darn good purpose.

By the way, chatting with the principal after the talk, I discovered that speaking to that group wasn't as sacred an honor as I had imagined. The schoolyear almost over, the students had already taken their end-of-semester exams, and the teachers simply needed something other than recess to fill the time. In fact, I found out that the next day another speaker would be talking about the Civil War. Who was this esteemed scholar entrusted to cover such an important historical topic, and impressive enough to follow such an impressive speaker as myself? None other than… the janitor.

SPEAKER SPONSORSHIPS

One of my most common speaking invitations has been for school-related events: academic achievement banquets, teacher in-services, end-of-semester time-fillers… Speakers at school events often aren't professionals. In fact, sometimes they're the freaking janitor. So if you're asked to speak at a school function, know that they'll expect you to do it for free.

Doing school talks pro bono is actually a great deal. Apart from the privilege of giving back, they're excellent experience and exposure. But a couple of years ago I discovered a way to get paid, too: speaker sponsorships.

What's a speaker sponsorship? A business serves as the paying "sponsor" for your talk. The school gets your speaking services for free, a business gets unique publicity (and partial credit for your awesome talk), and you get to add monetary compensation to the intangibles you're already receiving.

A good time to confirm that soliciting sponsorships is kosher is after you've discussed the school's expectations. Confirm the date, the time, the location, the topic, how long you'll have, whether they'll provide a projector, what kind of mic you'll be using, etc. Once everything's clear and settled, throw in, "By the way, sometimes I'll solicit speaker sponsorships for events like this. If one shows interest, would the school have any issue with me thanking them for sponsoring my talk?"

I've never had a school say no. And I suspect you won't either. But it's still good form to clear it with them at the outset.

Once it's confirmed, send out some mailers and/or make some calls to businesses you think might be interested, beginning with your bank and realtor. If one shows interest, settle on a fair fee, acquire their logo and what they'd like you to say, and rehearse delivering their mini-commercial as you rehearse everything else.

Ensure your sponsor is invited, and when the day comes, briefly preview your topic ("Today we join schools all across America as we honor our local veterans"), make your quick plug ("My talk is brought to you by Dixon Printing in Madisonville—go see Russ and Tabi on College Street for all your printing needs"), then transition into your material. The audience gets a quality talk, the school gets a free speaker, the sponsor gets a unique ad, and you get a taste of what it feels like to be a paid speaker.

You can of course do the speaker sponsor thing for any event, school-related or not. And if you're having trouble landing a sponsor, offer to recognize one for free. Dixon Printing, for example, hooked me up with some book promo banners, so I repaid the favor by recognizing them at that Vets Day program. Crediting a sponsor lets attendees know they can sponsor a future talk, gives you practice selling, and (if their business picks up) encourages them to be a paid sponsor next time.

BEGIN WHERE YOU ARE

Sponsorships are actually the second easiest way to get paid for speaking. Try polishing your authentic speaking self at your current job, where you're already getting paid by default. If the opportunities are rare, make some up—volunteer to lead a training or deliver a special announcement or liven up the company picnic with a comedy routine.

If your boss cramps your style (vetoing your visuals, demanding acronyms be spelled out, censoring your favorite Little Johnny joke), I can sympathize. It's hard to stay excited about speaking when fifteen different people are editing your presentation (fourteen of whom know nothing about effective presentation creation, let alone delivery), each pushing it further from something you can be proud of.

But if you can stand it, play their game, holding out hope that once they witness your burgeoning speaking prowess, your talks will be excused from the usual nitpicking. And to make their meddling palatable in the meantime, change what you must pre-talk, but make the delivery your own.

The Man may control the content, the order, and even the look. But you control your opening welcome, impromptu examples, word choice, and tone. If your creativity (aka your not safe for work sense of humor) is met with new requirements to follow a pre-approved script, don't give up. Just take your speaking ambition elsewhere.

Revisit the stretch assignments. Offer to host a workshop on something you enjoy. Volunteer to lead a special Sunday School class. When you feel ready (actually, before you feel completely ready), spread the word that you're available to keynote local events. As I've mentioned, my chamber of commerce has been immensely helpful for my speaking career, so consider working with yours. When you succeed, they succeed, so it's in their interests to help.

EASIER AT THE TOP?

However, don't settle for the small time. Patrick Schwerdtfeger, author of *Keynote Mastery: The Personal Journey of a Professional Speaker,* explains how the more intimidating opportunities are actually easier to score. Why? Because they tend to scare away the competition.

One thing that took his career to the next level was the ability to tout experience in exotic locations. Schwerdtfeger was amazed how accessible conferences in places like Denmark and Dubai were, largely because organizers wanted a speaker from the US and he was the only one applying. "So by going to the other side of the world, I had effectively eliminated my competition! I had no competitors. None. It blew my mind."

I've not applied to speak in Paris... yet. But I will. And you can bet that I'll tout it in my marketing materials once I do, and include the lessons learned in the third edition of this book.

So speak for free at first. Then find ways to do it at your nine-to-five, and give the sponsorship idea a try. If you continue to treat each engagement as a chance to improve, and each audience member as a potential client, soon enough you'll be in a position to negotiate direct fees, at which point you should invest in the speaking business books I've mentioned.

If life works out as it should, I'll be writing and speaking fulltime soon (sooner if you bless this book with a kind Amazon review, wink). In the meantime, catch me leading speaking workshops, emceeing retirement ceremonies, keynoting awards banquets and school events—enlightening, inspiring and entertaining—transferring cool ideas from my head into the heads of my audience members, and coaching brave rookies on how to do the same.

There was a time I couldn't have imagined getting paid to do this stuff. Know that if I can do it, so can you.

Key Takeaways

➲ Deliver **high quality** talks (this is *the* key)

➲ Consider every presentation a **job interview** (audience members are future clients)

➲ Please the person **paying the bill**

➲ Make your talk relevant to and about **your audience**

➲ Volunteer to speak at your **current job,** solicit **speaker sponsorships** for pro bono talks, then begin soliciting **direct payment gigs**

➲ You're a professional, polished speaker, so be open to getting paid to speak—**a win for you and your lucky clients**

➲ If after a school talk a teacher asks you to **mop up barf,** forgive them—honest mistake

Chapter Seventeen

TELL THEM WHAT YOU'VE TOLD THEM

You've covered a lot in a hurry—from the mind-body loop and the Urban Honey Badger, to the importance of tailoring your silent message and logically arranging your ideas, to handling tough crowds, be they standoffish or unruly. You know to rehearse as you intend to deliver, to engage your audience with stories, exercises, thought experiments, and emotionally potent examples, and to make eye contact with everyone except Mike Tyson.

Technology, scripts, voice, the speaking business—if it's been too much to absorb, just obey Elvis's ghost and stick to the Three Commandments: Know Thy Material, Be Thyself, and Practice. Get that much right, revisit relevant sections as you need them, and the rest will take care of itself.

Remember the basic truth that public speaking is communication—a matter of transferring ideas in your head into the heads of your audience members. Nothing mysterious or especially complicated about it. Accepting that fact, as well as your manageable role as expert and teacher, should release a great deal of unnecessary pressure.

Some of what you've learned has resonated. Some hasn't. Be like Bruce Lee—customize and internalize what works for you, and forget the rest. But one thing I hope you'll accept is my encouragement to begin speaking *now*.

People on their deathbeds don't lament the fact that they tried too hard, that they took too many risks, or that they pursued too many dreams too vigorously. No one says, "Boy, I sure am glad I played it safe." Rather, they say, "If only I could go back and do it again, I'd act more boldly. I'd take more chances. I wouldn't let fear stop me from attempting great things. I'd make more decisions based on love and hope, and fewer decisions based on what-if worry."

MR. JORDAN'S MANY FAILURES

There's an old Nike commercial in which Michael Jordan recounts his many failures.

I've missed more than nine thousand shots in my career. I've lost almost three hundred games. Twenty-six times, I've been trusted to take the game-winning shot and missed. I've failed over, and over, and over again in my life. And that is why I succeed.

On the surface, the point of the ad is that to achieve great things, you must endure great setbacks. But the underlying point (besides "buy Nike") is that winners don't let the fear of failure keep them from trying, and they don't let temporary setbacks keep them from improving.

Jordan didn't shy away from the chance to take his first game-winning shot because he might miss it. And he didn't refuse to take another game-winning shot when he had missed five, ten or even twenty-five.

Instead, he got back up, time and again, training harder and smarter (perfect practice makes perfect), working on areas within his control that delivered the biggest payoff (FM-AC), and practicing as he intended to perform. Jordan learned from his mistakes and built on his strengths. He didn't fade into obscurity, worried he might fail again. He constantly expanded his comfort zone by insisting, whether it was in high school, college, or the NBA, "Give me the ball. I got this."

A related quote from David Leddick's *I'm Not for Everyone. Neither Are You.*

I assure you when you have failed, if you fail, you are not going to go around kicking yourself. You will feel pretty good that you tried. You will say "There, that's out of the way. What's next?"

Leddick's right. My very first boxing bout was a loss—a split decision against a fighter half my age. Was I mortally embarrassed, destined to be an eternal loser in the ring, as well as life? On the contrary, I was as alive and as happy as I've ever been, proud for simply mustering the guts to step in the ring, and hungry to do it again. "It's like I was Rocky," I wrote in my journal. "Got to spit in a bucket between rounds and everything!"

For my next fight ("There, that's out of the way. What's next?"), not only did I enjoy the inner victory, but this time I got the external win, too. Ask to see my medal sometime, or my Fight of the Night trophy. They're on display in my home office (behind me as I write this), beneath pictures of me training with friends and family.

Some fights I won, some I lost. But regardless of the official outcome, I was always very much alive, growing, enjoying a dream I'd longed for (yet run from) for most of my life. I want that same fulfillment and satisfaction for you.

MR. ROOSEVELT'S AGELESS CALL

You've likely read or heard the following quote from Theodore Roosevelt, but I hope it speaks to your heart as powerfully now as it continues to speak to mine.

> It is not the critic who counts; not the man who points out how the strong man stumbles, or where the doer of deeds could have done them better. The credit belongs to the man who is actually in the arena, whose face is marred by dust and sweat and blood, who strives valiantly; who errs and comes short again and again; because there is no effort without error and shortcomings; but who does actually strive to do the deed; who knows the great enthusiasm, the great devotion, who spends himself in a worthy cause, who at the best knows in the end the triumph of high achievement and who at the worst, if he fails, at least he fails while daring greatly. So that his place shall never be with those cold and timid souls who know neither victory nor defeat.

Imagine what different lives Jordan and Roosevelt would have had if they'd allowed fear of failure to prevent them from pursuing great things. Imagine Mike the forklift driver or Teddy the baker, content—probably not, but fooling themselves—knowing full well they were hiding from their potential.

If you're already applying what you've learned, thank you. Thank you from me for making the writing (and revising) worthwhile. Thank you from your fellow humans for the ideas you're sharing and the value you're adding. And thank you from your future self for growing in such a cool, fulfilling way.

Alternatively, if you've read this entire book without speaking, or at least scheduling your next talk, now's the time. Not next week, not tomorrow, not later today. Fire up your email, pick up your phone, visit someone in person. Select an opportunity, sketch an outline, and commit to give a presentation within the next two weeks, *now*. (Wait, the library volunteer assignment is actually due by next Saturday at noon, so get busy.)

It doesn't matter if it's for one minute or one hour, on CPR or baking cookies, at work or the town hall. Commit now. Writing the goal down will transform it from a someday maybe wish into a *this* day inevitability. It will give you a reason to apply all you've learned. And you'll be *so* proud of yourself.

If you sincerely can't think of any opportunities to speak, think harder. If you still can't, drink some coffee. Then re-read chapter thirteen. And if you're still at a loss, visit a Toastmasters meeting.

TOASTMASTERS

Toastmasters is a wonderfully professional member-run organization that provides aspiring speakers a safe place to grow. Members meet on a regular schedule, complete a series of speaking assignments, and give one another high-quality, positive coaching in a quasi-formal environment. With regular rotation of the roles (General Evaluator, Time Keeper, Toastmaster of the Day), attendees also get a chance to develop their leadership. And from my experience, the senior folks are welcoming and eager to help newbies develop at their own pace. Nobody pushy, everyone helpful.

At your first meeting you can simply watch, but I encourage you to participate in their "Table Topics" exercise, where you'll give an impromptu two-minute talk on a topic randomly drawn from a hat. Table Topics talks always make me a little nervous, but that's why I love doing them. They're such a fantastic, low-stakes way to improve—huge payoff with very little risk. If it would help, I've prepared your opening and close for you:

Good morning/afternoon/evening—my name is [your name], and I'm going to give a brief presentation on [the random prompt]. [Answer the prompt by thinking out loud, elaborating on whatever comes to mind. This won't be perfect and that's OK. If you see a way to organize your ideas into 2-3 main points, go ahead. But just be honest and answer the prompt—everyone realizes you're doing this on the spot.] That's my brief presentation on [whatever]. Thanks so much for your attention.

The two minutes will be up before you know it, your classmates will clap and smile, and bam—you'll have completed your first impromptu speech.

Don't worry about how you'll do. Your peers will be aspiring speakers themselves, each at different stages of development. They'll know firsthand that the assignment isn't easy, and so will be extra proud of you for trying.

If you're not near a Toastmasters club, start your own. Just put the word out online or in the local newspaper, and meet every other week during lunch. Many employers, realizing the benefits for employee development, will authorize the space and time to start a chapter at work. All the info you need is at Toastmasters.org.

Or if you prefer, go independent. Find others interested in growing as speakers, settle on a time and place, and make it happen. Share your copy of this book, take turns presenting and coaching, helping one another customize and complete the Quick Wins, Stretch Assignments and Show Time assignments from chapter thirteen. Do it online if you prefer. No excuses. Get out there and present.

A FITTING CLOSE

Above all, the point that I hope you'll take away is one I've made many times in many ways: the key to realizing your enormous potential as a speaker is simply having the courage to get up there and the determination to improve. In that spirit, I'll encourage you now, just as I've encouraged you throughout, to get your nose out of the books and in front of an audience.

Sketch an outline for the checkout speech and commit to a specific date you'll deliver it. *Do it now.* Not next week, not tomorrow, not later today, but right now. It shouldn't take more than sixty seconds, and no matter your level of experience, it's completely doable. Or find that Toastmasters club. Or create your own. It'll be fun—promise.

As David Schwartz taught us, *action cures fear.* Overanalyzing fuels fear. Action destroys it. You'll be amazed how something as simple as sketching an outline will transform anxiety into anticipation, worry into momentum.

Then, as soon as you're *almost* ready—but not when you're completely ready (because that time will never come)—schedule the presentation that prompted you to study public speaking. Once you've done it, reflect on what went well, what didn't, improve, and dream bigger. Then bigger.

Roosevelt's nudge to live in the arena rather than spectate in the stands is a fitting close. Both a great speaker and a great person, he did things most go out of their way to avoid. And when he suffered setbacks, it bolstered his wisdom and strengthened his resolve.

Life's short. Let's not spend another moment on the sidelines. Focus where it matters and act where it counts. Pull the trigger on those dreams before you're fully ready. Put all you've learned into practice... *now*.

Do it for Elvis's ghost. Do it for Tron-freaking-Dareing. Do it *for you*.

If you enjoyed The *Best* Public Speaking Book, tell a friend or leave a brief review.

My readers (and listeners) are my marketing department. So thanks in advance.

And if you'd like to discuss anything, I'm not hard to find (MattDeaton.com).

More Books by Matt Deaton

Year of the Fighter:
Lessons from my Midlife Crisis Adventure
(2018)

★★★★★ ⌄   47 ratings

What it felt like to step in the ring for the first time, to do it against fighters half my age, and to sometimes win. The joys of getting kicked in the face, of being so exhausted (and possibly concussed) that I puked, and the self-coaching it took to make a lifelong dream a reality.

If achieving your potential as a speaker feels as intimidating as competitive fighting felt for me *(waaay* outside my comfort zone), check it out.

Ethics in a Nutshell:
The Philosopher's Approach to Morality in 100 Pages (2019)

★★★★½ ˅ 87 ratings

How philosophical ethics is compatible with religious moral reasoning, why moral relativism is untenable, with absurd implications, how to build and analyze moral arguments by analogy—stuff any good college ethics course would cover, plus accessible, concise, fun.

Find mini-lectures on each chapter (some at landmarks in New York, one floating down a river), teaching resources (sample syllabi, essay questions, vids on how to make your own vids), and even an "Ask Matt" interface at EthicsinaNutshell.org.

Abortion Ethics in a Nutshell:
A Pro-Both Tour of the Moral Arguments
(2021)

★★★★⯪ ˅   16 ratings

In the wake of the Dobbs decision, America needs a calm rethinking of abortion. And as most of us intuitively sense, it's too complicated for one favored "right" to override all other concerns.

Politicians and talking heads would have us believe we're either on Team Red or Team Blue with no room for thoughtful dissent. However, the inadequacy of the traditional paradigm becomes apparent via a simple yet illuminating exercise: "Rate That Abortion," the focus of chapter 4.

Ethics Bowl to the Rescue!
How the Anti-Debate is Saving Democracy
(coming 2022)

From Los Angeles to Long Island, Washington state to Washington, D.C., Texas to Tennessee, Ethics Bowls are a rising counter to the caustic, childish forces destroying civic discourse. Dubbed the "anti-debate" by Michigan High School Ethics Bowl organizer Jeanine DeLay, these transformative events are saving democracy, one person at a time.

Based on interviews with over two dozen coaches, organizers, judges and participants from as far away as Australia and China, learn why Ethics Bowl deserves its stellar reputation and your support.

P.S. All my books are now on audiobook.

So if you like listening or know someone who would enjoy the message, but treats books like kryptonite, find me at Amazon, Audible and iTunes.

Cheers, and thanks so much for reading.